CHILDHOOD AT COURT
1819–1914

ALSO BY JOHN VAN DER KISTE

Published by Sutton Publishing unless stated otherwise

Frederick III: German Emperor 1888 (1981)
Queen Victoria's Family: A Select Bibliography (Clover, 1982)
Dearest Affie: Alfred, Duke of Edinburgh, Queen Victoria's Second Son, 1844–1900 [with Bee Jordaan] (1984)
Queen Victoria's Children (1986; large print edition, ISIS, 1987)
Windsor and Habsburg: The British and Austrian Reigning Houses 1848–1922 (1987)
Edward VII's Children (1989)
Princess Victoria Melita: Grand Duchess Cyril of Russia, 1876–1936 (1991)
George V's Children (1991)
George III's Children (1992)
Crowns in a Changing World: The British and European Monarchies 1901–36 (1993)
Kings of the Hellenes: The Greek Kings 1863–1974 (1994)
Childhood at Court 1819–1914 (1995)
Northern Crowns: The Kings of Modern Scandinavia (1996)
King George II and Queen Caroline (1997)
The Romanovs 1818–1959: Alexander II of Russia and his Family (1998)
Kaiser Wilhelm II: Germany's Last Emperor (1999)
The Georgian Princesses (2000)
Gilbert & Sullivan's Christmas (2000)
Dearest Vicky, Darling Fritz: Queen Victoria's Eldest Daughter and the German Emperor (2001)
Royal Visits in Devon and Cornwall (Halsgrove, 2002)
Once a Grand Duchess: Xenia, Sister of Nicholas II [with Coryne Hall] (2002)
William and Mary (2003)

CHILDHOOD AT COURT 1819–1914

JOHN VAN DER KISTE

SUTTON PUBLISHING

This book was first published in 1995

This new revised paperback edition first published in 2003 by
Sutton Publishing Limited · Phoenix Mill
Thrupp · Stroud · Gloucestershire · GL5 2BU

British Library Cataloguing in Publication Data
A catalogue record for this book is available from the British
Library

ISBN 0 7509 3437 9

Typeset in 10/12pt Photina.
Typesetting and origination by
Sutton Publishing Limited.
Printed and bound in Great Britain by
J.H. Haynes & Co. Ltd, Sparkford.

Contents

Foreword

This book is an examination of the childhoods of royalty during the Victorian and Edwardian era. What were the education and upbringing of Queen Victoria and her descendants like, and how did it prepare them for the years ahead? What recreational pursuits and pets did they have? How much effect did tutors and governesses have on the Princes and Princesses? Was it a life of privilege and unbounded luxury? How did other children at court, such as the sons and daughters of members of the household, react to their glimpses of life at court? Were the days of their youth the happiest of their lives? To Princess Feodora, Queen Victoria's half-sister, childhood was 'that dismal existence of ours', while that of Queen Marie of Roumania was 'a happy, carefree one, the childhood of rich, healthy children protected from the buffets and hard realities of life'.

I have explored their lives, individually and collectively, in more or less chronological order, from the infancy of Queen Victoria herself to that of her great-grandchildren in the Edwardian age, taking the outbreak of the First World War as marking the end of the latter. Some might argue that to choose the date of birth of the Queen herself as the beginning of the Victorian age is taking liberties, but for this I offer no apology. While I have written on royal childhoods by families in some of my previous books, this new treatment is an attempt to throw new light on them – thanks in part to letters which were previously unavailable – and focus in greater detail than before, particularly on what might be termed the social and domestic, rather than biographical, aspects.

To cover the royal cousins in European reigning families of the age would have been impossible in a book of this size, but I have made allusion to the early years of some of the German and Russian imperial children, particularly where their paths crossed with their cousins in Britain.

Royal nicknames are used on occasion in the text, not in order to assume a false familiarity with the personages involved, so much as to try to minimize confusion between similarly named people and avoid perpetual use of the complete, sometimes rather cumbersome, title. Thus Prince Alfred, Duke of Edinburgh, is generally 'Affie', while his son is usually 'young Alfred' – as it so often was in the letters of Queen Victoria, equally keen to differentiate between the two.

I am grateful to the following for advice, assistance and access to previously unpublished material: the Trustees of the Broadlands Archives, Pat Bryan, Jim Hanson, Steven Jackson of the Commemorative Collectors Society, Ian Shapiro of Argyll Etkin Ltd, and Charlotte Zeepvat. Once again, the staff of the Kensington and Chelsea Public Libraries have generously allowed me access to their incomparable biography collection; my editors Jaqueline Mitchell and Rosemary Prudden have worked hard in seeing the work through to publication; and as ever my parents Wing Commander Guy and Nancy Van der Kiste have been an unfailing source of encouragement and help throughout.

1

'No scope for my very violent feelings of affection'

'Not to have enjoyed the pleasures of youth is nothing,' Princess Feodora of Hohenlohe-Langenburg wrote to her half-sister, Queen Victoria (17 March 1843), 'but to have been deprived of all intercourse, and not one cheerful thought in that dismal existence of ours, was very hard.'[1]

'Our childhood was a happy, carefree one,' Princess Marie of Edinburgh, later Queen Marie of Roumania, wrote in contrast some ninety years later, 'the childhood of rich, healthy children protected from the buffets and hard realities of life.'[2]

Princess Victoria of Kent, who succeeded to the throne as Queen Victoria less than a month after her eighteenth birthday, had a comparatively deprived childhood. Most of her grandchildren, including Queen Marie of Roumania, grew up as one child of several in a large nursery. So did many of her subjects, among them Molly Hughes: 'A girl with four brothers older than herself is born under a lucky star. To be brought up in London, in the eighteen-seventies, by parents who knew how to laugh at both jokes and disasters, was to be under the influence of Jupiter.'[3]

Queen Victoria was never under the influence of Jupiter. Her father married for reasons of state, to a widow nearly nineteen years younger than himself; only a long journey by her parents when her mother was seven months pregnant ensured that she was born on British soil; her christening was the scene of a family quarrel which had her mother in tears; and she was a mere eight months old when her father died.

On 6 November 1817 Princess Charlotte, wife of Prince Leopold of Saxe-Coburg Saalfeld and daughter of George, Prince Regent, died in childbirth after producing a stillborn son. The prospects for

1

the British line of succession were ominous. None of the thirteen sons and daughters of King George III and Queen Charlotte who survived to maturity had produced a single legitimate child among them, with the exception of the hapless Princess Charlotte. It was vital for the King's bachelor sons to contract officially recognized marriages and ensure the succession – with the bait of generous marriage grants. Since most of them were better at spending money than saving it, such offers were irresistible.

On 30 May 1818 the King's fourth son Edward, Duke of Kent, married the widowed Princess Victoire of Leiningen at the Ehrenburg Palace, Coburg. Aged thirty-one, she had two children by her marriage to Emich Charles, Prince of Leiningen, Prince Charles and Princess Feodora. In order to prevent doubts as to the validity of the marriage, and succession problems in either country – as the King of Great Britain was also King of Hanover – a second ceremony was held at Kew Palace on 11 July. The latter was a double wedding, the union between William, Duke of Clarence and Princess Adelaide of Saxe-Meiningen being solemnized at the same time.

Marriage, and a parliamentary grant, did not put an end to the Duke of Kent's financial problems. On the contrary, it intensified them. He had increased his debts by borrowing to pay for presents to his wife, including a splendid wedding dress. The Prince Regent, no novice at the art of spending lavishly himself and no friend of his radically minded brother, refused to help him. The rest of the family urged the Kents to leave the country, since living abroad was cheaper, and in September they returned to Amorbach.

Within weeks, the Duchess knew that she was with child. Like his newly married brothers, the Duke had lost no time in obeying the call of duty. Convinced that the irregular lives of his brothers would ensure that his children would rule over England one day, the Duke realized how vital it was for his first-born child to be born in England. That the Clarences, who were higher in the succession than the Kents, were preparing for their confinement in Hanover, carried no weight with him. A few friends lent him sufficient money to return to England, and in March 1819 they set out on their journey.

The Duchess of Kent was seven months pregnant as they began their 427-mile odyssey, the Duke driving her and his stepdaughter

Feodora in a cane phaeton over rough roads, in order to save the expense of hiring a coachman. The motley procession also comprising a landau, a barouche, two large post-chaises, a cabriolet and a caravan, reached Calais and had to wait a week for favourable conditions at sea. On 24 April they crossed the Channel; the Duchess was very sick on the journey, but according to Madame Siebold, an obstetrician in the suite, there were no harmful symptoms. They settled at Kensington Palace, and after a labour of more than six hours, at 4.15 on the morning of 24 May the Duchess gave birth to a daughter. The father had remained at her side throughout, while the Duke of Wellington, Archbishop Manners Sutton, and other privy councillors, waited in an adjoining room. It was their duty to ensure that no suppositious infant could be smuggled into the bed.

Madame Siebold was responsible for helping to bring the Princess into the world. Also in attendance at the birth was a Welsh doctor, Dr David Daniel Davis. Legend has it that the labour was so difficult that Madame Siebold gave up hope of saving either mother or child, and Dr Davis had to intervene. This was untrue. Madame Siebold was a foreigner and a German, and the Duke of Kent had been advised that it would bode better for his popularity if a well-known British obstetrician was on hand at the same time, just in case anything should go wrong.

The Duke was overjoyed, writing that evening to his mother-in-law, the Dowager Duchess of Coburg, that her new grandchild was 'truly a model of strength and beauty combined. . . . Thank God the dear mother and the child are doing marvellously well.'[4]

For the first three weeks, their existence seemed blissfully happy. The Duke had been only momentarily disappointed that his firstborn child had not been a son, declaring that 'the decrees of Providence are at all times wisest and best'. The Duchess was determined not to engage a wet-nurse, but breast-fed the child herself. The Duke, who took an intense interest in all details of nursery management, observed 'the process of maternal nutriment' with fascination.

The constant shadow that spoilt the proud father's state of happiness was not slow to appear. As he knew only too well, the Prince Regent was determined to make life uncomfortable for the family. He had never forgiven the Duke of Kent for the sympathy he had shown to his estranged wife Caroline, the Princess of Wales, who had since retired abroad. That the Wales's only child Charlotte had died prematurely while the Kents' daughter appeared healthy enough was a further source of bitterness and resentment on the part of the Prince Regent. The Duchess of Clarence had also given birth to a daughter in March, a sickly baby who only lived for seven hours. To the Prince Regent, his detested brother Edward had evidently been born under a lucky star.

As acting head of the family, in lieu of the blind, insane King George III, the Prince Regent decided when the christening of the Princess should take place. On 21 June the Duke of Kent was abruptly notified by the Prince's private secretary and privy seal, Sir Benjamin Bloomfield, of the arrangements. The ceremony would be three days later, on 24 June, at 3.00 p.m. It would be held privately, with only the Duke and Duchess of York, Princess Augusta, the Duke and Duchess of Gloucester, Prince Leopold and Princess Sophia invited as family guests. There would be no chance of the Duke of Kent being allowed to make a grand occasion of the ceremony. No foreign dignitaries would be invited to add pomp and splendour to the occasion. The Prince Regent would stand as godparent in person, Tsar Alexander I of Russia would be represented by the Duke of York, then second in succession to the throne, and the remaining godparents by other members of the royal family. The parents were not even permitted to choose the names themselves, which the Prince Regent 'will explain himself to your Royal Highness, previous to the Ceremony'.[5]

No more was heard from the Prince Regent until the evening before the christening. A list of names had been submitted to him, and it was assumed that he would raise no objection, but on Sunday evening he sent a message to the Duke of Kent that the name Georgina was not to be used, as the Regent did not wish to place his name before that of the Tsar of Russia, and he could not allow it to come afterwards. With regard to the other names, he would speak to the Duke of Kent at the ceremony. Unknown to the parents, he had already approached Prince Leopold, asking him to prevent the name Charlotte from being given.

When the modest company assembled in the Cupola Room at Kensington Palace the next day the Regent, determined to be as cold as possible, did not exchange a single word with the Duke of

Kent. As the Archbishop of Canterbury held the Princess in his arms, waiting for the Regent to pronounce the first name, he announced gruffly, 'Alexandrina'. He then stopped, and the Archbishop waited. The Duke of Kent suggested Charlotte, Augusta, and Elizabeth. All these met with fierce disapproval from his brother, who coldly said she could be baptized with her mother's name, 'but it cannot precede that of the Emperor'. By the time Princess Alexandrina Victoria of Kent had been christened, the Duchess of Kent was sobbing.

That evening the Duke and Duchess gave a dinner party at Kensington Palace. Not surprisingly, the Prince Regent was not invited.

The Princess was regularly known among the family as 'Drina', though she and her mother preferred the name Victoria. As a baby, her mother called her 'Vickelchen', and lulled her to sleep each night with German cradle songs.

On 2 August 1819 she became the first royal baby to be vaccinated against smallpox. The six-week-old child of Colonel Eliot, MP, was brought to Kensington Palace. Vaccine lymph was taken from the vesicle, the cavity filled with pus resulting from the insertion of the vaccine on the arm of Colonel Eliot's child, and inserted into two places on the Princess's left arm and one on her right. By the twenty-sixth day after vaccination, the scabs had dropped off, leaving 'a small radiated and rather depressed cicatrix'. The vaccination had been successful, and the Princess suffered no side-effects.

Although bitterly resented by the brother who was King in all but name, the Duke of Kent, his wife and child were leading an apparently contented life. Their cosy domesticity was the subject of some gentle mockery on the part of Mary, Duchess of Gloucester, who noted that on a visit to Windsor in September they retired to bed at the almost unheard-of-hour of 9 p.m.

Yet financial troubles continued to dog the family, and pursue the father to his grave – if not indirectly lead him to it. The Duke of Kent could not afford to live in London; to economize, it was necessary to live somewhere in the country. Returning to Germany, which would at least take them out of sight of resentful relatives, would be too expensive, and as he was determined that his daughter (and perhaps he himself before her) would one day ascend the throne, it would not do for them to go back into self-imposed exile.

A suggestion was made that they should visit, perhaps stay in, Devonshire. This would be a good way of preserving appearances, as the Duke had announced his intention of taking the Duchess to benefit from sea air after her confinement. He and his equerry, Captain John Conroy, went to look at houses in Dawlish, Torquay, Teignmouth and Sidmouth. Between them they decided that Sidmouth would be most satisfactory, and they rented Woolbrook Cottage, close to the seafront.

On 2 November, back at Kensington Palace, the Duke celebrated his fifty-second birthday with what was rather grandly described as a 'family festival'. This consisted of the presentation of a letter written by the Duchess and presented to him by the Princess, now aged five months, dressed in a white frock with bows of red and green ribbon, and wearing a Scottish bonnet. Princess Feodora sang some verses composed for the occasion, and from his school in Geneva Prince Charles of Leiningen wrote a letter in English to 'please my dear father', sending 'filial congratulations'.

On 3 December 1819 one of the decisive influences on the Princess's early life arrived at Kensington Palace. Louise Lehzen, the daughter of a Lutheran clergyman in the village of Lagenhagen, Hanover, was engaged by the Duke of Kent to become governess to Princess Feodora. He intended that she should also become Princess Victoria's governess when her nurse, Mrs Brock, left. Thirty-five years old, Fraulein Lehzen had been governess to three daughters in the von Marenholtz family. Highly recommended, and described by diarist Charles Greville as 'a clever agreeable woman', her strength of personality would lead to some stormy scenes within the next couple of decades.

Later that month the entourage set out for Devon. Breaking their journey at Salisbury, they toured the Cathedral and the Duke caught a heavy cold. Although the winter of 1819 to 1820 proved unusually cold, with rain and gales adding to the rigours of exceptionally low temperatures, he refused to fuss, insisting that he would outlive all his brothers. They arrived at Sidmouth on the afternoon of Christmas Day in a fierce snowstorm.

The rest of the family also caught severe colds, and on 28 December while sitting in the drawing room with the infant

Princess, the Duchess was terrified as a shot shattered the window. The culprit was a local apprentice boy named Hook, who had been shooting birds. Despite their alarm, the Duke and Duchess made light of the incident. Relieved that it was not some underhand assassination attempt, the Duke observed that his daughter had stood fire as befitted a soldier's daughter. Meanwhile they asked Conroy to write to the local magistrates, asking them to help ensure the prevention of such an occurrence, but requesting particularly that the boy should not be punished.

On 6 January 1820 the Duke wrote to Admiral Donnelly, whose house he had occupied in Brussels, enquiring about arrangements for returning to Amorbach in the spring. In the same letter he observed that 'our little Girl now between seven and eight months looks like a child of a year, and has cut her two first teeth without the slightest inconvenience'.[6]

It was the last letter he ever wrote. Despite his cold, he insisted on going out walking in all weathers. Returning one evening chilled and soaked through, he refused to change his boots. Within a few days his chill had turned to high fever, delirium and vomiting. Medical attention could do little to alleviate his sufferings. On the morning of 23 January he passed away.

The disconsolate, fatherless family returned to Kensington Palace. On their journey the carriages were very bad, and, the Duchess wrote to her confidante, Polyxene von Tubeuf, 'poor little Vickelchen got very upset by the frightful jolting'.[7] Returning to Kensington, they learned that King George III's phantom existence had come to an end. Outliving his fourth son by six days, he died on 29 January aged eighty-one.

Widowed for the second time, with daughters aged twelve years and eight months, living in a strange country whose language she could scarcely speak, the Duchess of Kent was sorely tempted to return to Germany. Only the insistence of her brother Prince Leopold persuaded her to settle permanently in England. For the next seventeen years she would oversee the childhood of the woman who would give her name to the age.

The childhood of Queen Victoria was anything but luxurious. Not only did she lack a father, but she had very few of the creature comforts which her uncles or aunts had known, or indeed which her children were to enjoy: 'I never had a room to myself; I never had a sofa, nor an easy chair; and there was not a single carpet that was not threadbare.'[8]

Her education began, tentatively, when she was four years old. The Revd George Davys, who took services in Kensington Palace Chapel, was her first tutor. He started with a box of letters and some coloured cards, on which he wrote simple words, and placed them around the room. He then called out a word and the Princess had to find it with the aid of the letters.

'I was not fond of learning as a little child,' the Queen recalled in 1872, 'and baffled every attempt to teach me my letters up to 5 years old – when I consented to learn them by their being written down before me.'[9]

So many legends have grown up about her education, with frequently conflicting stories about her childhood published within her lifetime, that one is grateful for her recollections, and the fact that she annotated several of the inaccurate accounts in her own hand. For example, it has often been accepted as fact that she heard only German spoken until the age of three, when she began to learn English.[10] When presented with a copy of Miss Agnes Strickland's *Victoria from Birth to Bridal*, published in 1840, she found mention of the 'fact' that 'many caressing phrases were addressed by the little Princess to her Royal Mother in German'. In the margin, she wrote, 'Not true. Never spoke German until 1839, not allowed to. Not true her mother stimulated her to speak German.'[11]

The educational process began in earnest in 1827, when she was eight years old, and Davys was appointed her Principal Master. A regular timetable was drawn up for her. Morning lessons were from 9.30 to 11.30 a.m., after which she was allowed to play or go for a walk until dinner at 1 p.m. Afternoon lessons, which included drawing, lasted from 3 to 5 p.m., after which she learnt poetry by heart for an hour, in English, French and German. Wednesday afternoons were given over to learning her catechism, and religious instruction from Davys. On Thursday she had her dancing lesson, and on Friday morning she was taught music and singing by Mr Sale, the organist at St Margaret's, Westminster. She had a soprano voice, 'not powerful but remarkably sweet and true'.

On Saturday the hours were shorter. She went over the lessons she had learned during the week till 11 a.m. and was then free until a German lesson at 3 p.m.; from 4 to 5 p.m. she wrote letters and from 5 to 6 p.m. had French repetition. The Duchess of Kent stated that she herself 'almost always . . . attended every lesson or a part', an assertion that her daughter later vehemently denied. Although the Queen insisted that she was 'not allowed to' speak German until 1839, a rather strange remark in view of the fact that by then she had been on the throne for two years, the accounts of others make it evident that she began learning the language at an early age – even if she was apparently not allowed to speak it.

Brought up in the Church of England, the Princess could repeat her catechism by the time she was eleven, and had a thorough understanding of the principal doctrines of the Church of England.

Great emphasis was placed on modern languages. Her French tutor, M. Grandineau, was very impressed with her progress. When she was ten, he reported that she could carry on a conversation in French; her grammar was excellent and her accent would eventually be perfect, though she did not write French as well as she spoke. Her German tutor was the Revd Henry Barez, a Lutheran clergyman, who reported that at the same age she had acquired 'a correct German pronunciation, particularly remarkable for its softness and distinctness'. She constantly studied a German grammar which had been specially written for her. Davys also taught her Latin, with the aid of a standard contemporary grammar produced particularly for the boys of Eton, but she found the subject difficult and 'was not so far advanced'.

Her writing master, Mr Steward, also taught her arithmetic. He considered she had a particular talent for it, working out sums correctly and understanding his explanation of the rules. In geography and history, also under Davys, she was 'better informed than most young persons of the same age'. She read poetry aloud 'extremely well', and had a talent for drawing. Good deportment was regarded as essential, and in order to make her sit up straight, a sprig of holly was pinned to the front of her dress just under her chin.

Lehzen read aloud to her while she was dressing and while her hair was being brushed. Only educational and informative books were permitted, fiction not being allowed. For the first twenty years or so of the nineteenth century, only 'improving books' were considered suitable for children. Works of 'fiction and fancy' were deemed a bad influence, particularly adventure stories, most of which featured either war, piracy or murder, and thus infected the young mind with harmful ideas. Only stories with a moral, in which marvellous things happened to the good child and dreadful things to the terrible one, were approved.

The Princess's greatest failing was inattention, described politely by the tutors as 'absence of mind'. Reports produced for the Duchess of Kent were, not surprisingly, quite flattering; to some extent, the tutors' future employment depended on proof that they were doing their job properly, but the Princess was not a model pupil. Like many schoolgirls before and since she disliked learning, and looked forward eagerly to 'holly days'.

In 1827 she had her first drawing lesson from Richard Westall. From then until his death nine years later, he called at Kensington Palace twice a week to give her lessons lasting about an hour. He taught her drawing and sketching, but not painting in oils. He had also illustrated modern editions of Goethe's *Faust*, Byron's *Don Juan*, and Walter Scott's poems, although his pictures lacked the imagination and energy of those by artists of the previous generation such as William Blake and Henry Fuseli. Princess Victoria was his first, and only, pupil, and she faithfully copied his drawings of hands, eyes and horses. Although he supported a blind sister on his meagre income, he declined to accept any payment for the lessons he gave the Princess, though his sister received some financial assistance from the Duchess of Kent.

Romantic ballet and opera were all the rage in London during the 1820s and '30s, and Princess Victoria was an enthusiastic patron. She might be taken to Covent Garden by her mother, Lehzen and the Conroys two or three times a week in spring to see a show. She was particularly taken with *La Sylphide*, danced by Marie Taglioni, 'like a fawn', on a set made more magnificent by its revolutionary use of gas lighting. She also saw the most celebrated interpreters of Italian opera on the stage, performing works by Bellini, Meyerbeer, Rossini and Donizetti. At the same time she was brought up to appreciate drama, and Shakespeare productions starring Edmund Kean and Fanny Kemble were a vital part of her education as well as providing entertainment value.

Her best friends were her dolls, substitutes for the girl companions she was never allowed. She did not care for babies, and her dolls were not the small children that little girls of the day liked to play with and act as mother to. They were miniature adult dolls, mostly representing characters from plays and operas that she had seen. She and Lehzen dressed them and kept them in a box. A list of 132 was kept, mentioning the name of each, and the characters they represented. Among them were Amy Brocard (the Countess of Leicester) and Zoe Beaupré (Queen Elizabeth). They were quite ordinary, varying in height from three to nine inches, with the 'Dutch doll'* type of face, easy to pack away. Collecting them was the chief outlet for her affection and imagination, and she played at 'teaching' them the manners she had been taught herself. This remained a favourite amusement until she was nearly fourteen years old.

She could be extremely possessive about them. When Lady Radnor came to call on the Duchess of Kent, she brought her granddaughter Jane to play with the Princess. 'The young Princess quickly and warningly told me, referring to toys scattered around "You must not touch those, they are mine; and I may call you Jane, but you must not call me Victoria."'[12]

Firmly supervised by her elders, the Princess led a lonely childhood, isolated from her contemporaries most of the time. Until her accession to the throne she slept in her mother's room. When she had been put to bed in the evening, Lehzen sat in the room until the Duchess came to retire. She was never allowed to see anyone, young or old, unless a third person was present. For several years she was not allowed to walk downstairs without someone holding her hand.

This heavily cocooned existence was for long taken as an example of excessive parental control and an attempt to make her psychologically over-dependent on her mother and staff. It has also, more charitably, been put down to the Duchess of Kent's sense of insecurity, her hostility to her brothers-in-law and mistrust of what she saw as their conspiratorial motives. This

---

*Jointed wooden dolls, usually carved from pinewood in Germany and Austria, named thus as a corruption of 'deutsch', or according to another theory as they were imported into England via Holland. They were succeeded by papier-mâché dolls, which could be moulded and easily painted, and, from about 1830, dolls with porcelain or glazed china heads.

insecurity, it is alleged, also resulted in her 'obsessive treasuring of everything associated with her child'.[13] After the Duchess of Kent's death in 1861, this daughter was overcome at discovering that not a scrap of her writing or hair had ever been thrown away, in addition to a book containing 'such touching notes about her babyhood'.

For the first few years she had the companionship of her half-sister, Princess Feodora ('Fidi'). The latter was sent off to Germany to stay with her grandmother when she was nineteen, possibly to escape the unwelcome attention of King George IV who, as gossips suggested, was even considering a royal remarriage at this late stage in his life, in order to produce an heir to the throne. The thought of this ailing recluse of a monarch marrying a Princess some forty-five years his junior seems far-fetched, but at any rate Feodora was despatched out of harm's way back to the land of her birth, and in 1827 her betrothal to Prince Ernest of Hohenlohe-Langenburg was announced.

The departure of her one close contemporary increased Princess Victoria's isolation, and threw her increasingly onto her dolls for company. Her only occasional playmate was John Conroy's daughter Victoire, who was only a few months older than the Princess. Victoire was treated coldly, as the daughter of a man whom the Princess hated and despised, and there was never any closeness between the two.

In the last few years of her life, an exhibition of the Queen's dolls was staged. She recalled her devotion to them, as '*she* was an *only* child and except occasional visits of other children lived always *alone*, without companions. Once a week one child came.'[14]

Apart from her dolls, the other great playthings at her disposal were mechanical toys made in Nuremburg. One was a hand-loom, twenty-two inches long, on which jute could be woven into coarse cloth. Another, less didactic but surely more fun, was a miniature clockwork roadway with an avenue of little trees, on which a doll, two and a half inches high, moved along grooved lines. Two lines ran parallel; small pagoda-shaped buildings at either end partly concealed the action of the puppet as it turned into the path parallel with the one just traversed.

The Princess's favourite was a miniature stage, eight inches long and three inches wide. The curtain drew back to reveal three figures, brilliantly dressed in silks and satins, dancing and pirouetting animatedly to the tinkling of a musical box concealed underneath. It was enclosed in a neat rosewood box shaped like an upright piano. A leather strap for suspension went round the neck of the owner, when she was 'playing at being showman'.

Among other toys which doubtless found their way into Kensington Palace were simple jigsaws, or 'dissected puzzles'. These hand-coloured engravings, mounted on wood, were already well established as recreational favourites for young children. Their educational role was taken seriously; the subjects of such puzzles were usually themes such as the kings and queens, or counties, of England, or the countries of Europe. A variation on these was the 'race game', an early nineteenth-century forerunner of Snakes & Ladders and other board games. 'Virtue Rewarded and Vice Punished' was a popular example. The players had to compete to see who would be the first to reach The Cottage of Content, by landing on steps such as Patience Pond, Lucky Lane or Forethought Road en route, and avoiding Laughing Stock Lane (Pay 2 for laughing) and Frog Island (Pay 1 for frightening the frogs). These games of chance might be played with counters and dice. If parents and guardians wished to avoid introducing impressionable young minds to dice, a harmful influence as they were gambling tools which would lead the children into bad ways, the use of a teetotum, or multi-sided spinning top, was recommended as an alternative.

Every summer Princess Victoria would be taken to Ramsgate, Tunbridge Wells, or somewhere similar on or near the coast. It made a pleasant change from Kensington Palace, and the return home each autumn 'was generally a day of tears'. Ramsgate was always remembered with affection. Living next to the house the Duchess rented was the philanthropist Moses Montefiore, who had retired from his banking career at the age of forty to devote the rest of his life to good causes. He presented the Princess with a small gold key to his garden gate, with an open invitation to use it whenever she wished.

To outside observers the little girl seemed happy enough. Lord Albemarle, at that time a servant of the Princess's uncle the Duke of Sussex, would recall in later years watching from his window the movements of a vivacious, attractive little girl, seven years of age, wearing a large straw hat, and a suit of white cotton. 'It was amusing to see how impartially she divided the contents of the watering pot between the flowers and her own little feet.'[15]

After dining one day with the Duchess, the diarist Harriet Arbuthnot, wife of a Cabinet official, wrote that Princess Victoria was the most charming child she had ever seen, with high spirits, but civil and well bred. The Duchess was 'a very sensible person & educates her remarkably well'.

As a grown woman Queen Victoria never glossed over the misery of her early years. Writing to her eldest daughter Victoria on 9 June 1858, five months after her marriage to Prince Frederick William of Prussia, she recalled: 'I had led a very unhappy life as a child – had no scope for my very violent feelings of affection – had no brothers and sisters to live with – never had had a father – from my unfortunate circumstances was not on a comfortable or at all intimate footing with my mother (so different from you to me) – much as I love her now – and did not know what a happy domestic life was!'[16]

Princess Feodora sympathized with her plight more than anyone. 'I escaped some years of imprisonment, which you, my poor darling sister, had to endure after I was married,'[17] she wrote in 1843.

The Duchess of Kent was, and always remained, a stranger in a strange land. It was only natural for her to lean increasingly on the man whom her second husband had appointed to the household so soon after their marriage. Unfortunately, this particular man drove a wedge between mother and daughter, and the effects lasted for some years after he had gone from their lives for ever.

John Conroy was in effect the ruler of all that went on at Kensington Palace. An ambitious, unscrupulous, scheming man, he saw that as chief unofficial counsellor to the Duchess of Kent, he could surely exert similar control over the future Queen of England, and if he was patient would doubtless reap what he considered his just reward for years of royal service. When the Duke of York, King George IV's heir to the throne, died in January 1827, only two lives stood between the crown and the seven-year-old Princess – the King himself, who could not be expected to survive long in his wretched state of health, and the eccentric, excitable Duke of Clarence. The latter still had no legitimate children to succeed him, despite the Duchess's tragic history of miscarriages, still births, and babies who lived for only a few weeks. He was aged sixty-one, and if gossips were to be believed, he was becoming subject to the same lack of mental stability that had blighted the last years of King George III's life. If Princess Victoria ascended the throne before the age of eighteen, a regency would be necessary. The Duchess of Kent would be nominally Regent, but Conroy would be the power behind the throne.

With this in mind, he devised the 'Kensington System', designed to make the Princess utterly dependent on her mother. He had already played his part in separating the half-sisters by helping to bring about the betrothal of Princess Feodora, who married less for love than to escape from Kensington Palace. With her departure, Conroy – now Sir John, newly created a Knight Commander of the Hanoverian Order by King George IV in his capacity as King of Hanover – and the Duchess now had the Princess to themselves. Lehzen, now Baroness Lehzen, would doubtless remember that she owed her well-being entirely to her employers, and do exactly as she was required. The Princess was accordingly to be kept isolated within the Kensington circle, and no risk could be taken of anybody from outside winning her affections and undermining her mother's authority. Conroy was fiercely ambitious, notoriously short-tempered and totally insensitive. He was also too stupid, or too impatient, to make any effort to gain the Princess's affection or respect.

In the autumn of 1829 Baroness Späth, the Duchess of Kent's devoted lady-in-waiting, was dismissed. Years of selfless service to the Duchess and then her daughter counted for nothing against her one crime – to stand up to Conroy. She and Lehzen had resented his high-handed behaviour and his insistence on giving Lady Conroy precedence at court over them; she had also tried to put Victoire Conroy, very much her father's daughter, in her place.* Späth was banished on the grounds that it was necessary to surround the Princess with ladies of English rank, rather than Germans; that she expressed 'adverse opinions' about the

---

*Allegations that Princess Victoria had witnessed over-familiar behaviour between Conroy and the Duchess of Kent, and spoken to Späth who then remonstrated with Conroy, remain unproved.

Kensington system; and that she spoiled Princess Victoria by too much adulation.

The Princess had been very fond of Späth, and doted on Lehzen. Conroy attempted to dismiss the latter as well, but King George IV and the Duke of Clarence were warned what was happening, and they insisted that she should stay where she was, on the grounds that her departure would be harmful to the Princess.

On 10 March 1830 the Bishop of London asked the Duchess of Kent if the Princess knew what was likely to be her future station in the country, and would her education be planned to put her in possession of this knowledge? The Duchess said that she had not yet made up her mind to tell the Princess she would be Queen, hoping she would come across the knowledge 'by accident, in pursuing her education'.

Possibly by coincidence, or more probably by design, all was revealed the following day. Though it sounds apocryphal, the truth of the 'I will be good' episode was confirmed some thirty-seven years later in written recollections by Baroness Lehzen, and endorsed, for the most part, by Queen Victoria. The ten-year-old Princess opened a book, Howlett's *Tables of the Kings and Queens of England*, to begin her history lesson with Lehzen. She found with some surprise that an extra page had been slipped into the book. It was a genealogical table showing recent heirs to the throne, all descended from her grandfather King George III, with the date of death where applicable written after each name. She studied it carefully, coming to the names of her uncles King George IV and William, Duke of Clarence – followed by her own. After some thought, she said solemnly, 'I see I am nearer to the throne than I thought,' and burst into tears. After recovering her composure, she said to Lehzen, 'Now – many a child would boast but they don't know the difficulty; there is much splendour, but there is more responsibility!' Lifting up the forefinger of her right hand, she uttered the famous words, 'I will be good.'[18]

The story sounds too much like legend, and in her old age Lehzen undoubtedly added her own touch of drama to the recollections. Such phrases sound rather beyond all but the most precocious infant of ten. As her biographer Monica Charlot has suggested, the language seems stilted and unchildlike, and from other accounts the young princess did not seem such a prig as this story makes out. Moreover, the veracity of the account is open to question, as it is in effect a reconstruction long after the event.[19] Nevertheless Queen Victoria, whose powers of recall remained remarkably sharp well into her later years, and who was always eager to dismiss sugary stories about her childhood, never rejected this one. On the margin of Lehzen's memoirs, she wrote, 'I cried much on learning it and ever deplored this contingency.'

In June 1830 King George IV died at Windsor, and the Duke of Clarence ascended the throne as King William IV. It was now obvious to all but the most optimistic that his consort, now Queen Adelaide, would never produce a healthy heir to the throne, and increasingly inevitable that Princess Victoria of Kent would succeed him.

The new King and Queen were well disposed enough towards the Duchess of Kent and fond of her daughter, though they were suspicious of Conroy's influence at Kensington Palace. Princess Victoria had not been allowed the close acquaintance with her kindly uncle and aunt that she would have liked, though she knew enough about the Queen's tragic attempts at motherhood to hope that she would have the child she craved. The Duchess of Kent kept her daughter away from the 'Acquatics' as she contemptuously dubbed them, because – it was said – she looked askance at King William IV's illegitimate brood, the adult children of his long liaison with the late actress Dorothy Jordan. The distance she put between herself and her brother- and sister-in-law, however, was part and parcel of Conroy's plan of keeping the Kents in splendid isolation, under his influence.

In July 1830 Princess Victoria attended a Garter ceremony at St James's Palace, and her small, withdrawn figure in black veil and weepers reaching to the ground, walking behind Queen Adelaide, was commented on by the German Ambassador. The next month, she was invited to court for the celebrations of Queen Adelaide's thirty-eighth birthday. Though happy to be at the festivities, she was ill at ease and too frightened of her mother's anger to smile and appear too friendly. King William complained later that she had stared at him stonily.

If the King had had his way, Princess Victoria would not have been called thus for much longer. Soon after Christmas, he instructed his Prime Minister, Lord Grey, to tell the Duchess of Kent that he wanted the Princess's name to be changed to an English one. As the girl bore an Anglicized version of her mother's name, Victoire, the request was hardly a tactful one, but the King stood by 'his sole aim being that the name of the future Sovereign of this country should be *English*'. Elizabeth and Charlotte were mentioned as possible alternatives. With reluctance, the Archbishop of Canterbury informed that it might be legally possible to change a name by Act of Parliament, but the Duchess put up such a show of resistance that the idea was soon dropped.

It was a portent of clashes to come. The Duchess and her daughter were commanded to attend the Coronation in September 1831, and Princess Victoria was to be assigned a place in the procession behind the surviving Royal Dukes. As heiress presumptive, the Duchess of Kent maintained that her daughter should be allowed to walk directly behind the sovereign. Neither side would give way, and the Duchess refused to attend the ceremony or allow the Princess to participate, making excuses that they could not afford the expense, and that she feared the strain on her daughter's health. The Princess was bitterly disappointed. Nothing, she recalled later, could console her – not even her dolls.

In 1832, shortly after her thirteenth birthday, two important changes took place in the life of the young Princess. She was instructed to keep a diary, which she maintained almost without ceasing until within a few days of her death sixty-eight years later; and she began to undertake extensive travels throughout the country.

The semi-royal tours, or 'progresses', to acquaint her with the country and with her future subjects, were instituted by Conroy. They were arranged without the consent of King William IV, whose entourage at court was predominantly Tory, while that of the Duchess of Kent was mainly Whig. Only too happy to exploit the emotions aroused by the year of the Great Reform Bill, Conroy encouraged citizens to present loyal addresses containing references to the Duchess's support for the 'free people' of England.

Immediately before the first of these journeys, the Princess was presented with a small leather-backed notebook with mottled covers. The first inscription reads: 'This Book Mama gave me that I might write the journal of my journey to Wales in it. Victoria,

Kensington Palace, July 31st.'[20] The Princess's pencil writing is inked over by an adult hand.

The initial entries were no more than a dry record of events. Meant for the approval of her governess and her mother, they could hardly contain anything that was not strictly factual. The first entry, for Wednesday 1 August 1832, records rather mechanically that

> We left K[ensington] P[alace] at 6 minutes past 7 and went through the Lower-field gate to the right. We went on, & turned to the left by the new road to Regent's Park. The road & scenery is beautiful. 20 minutes to 9. We have just changed horses at Barnet, a very pretty little town.[21]

Passing through the Midlands, near Birmingham she had her first sight of industrial England:

> We just passed through a town where all coal mines are and you see the fire glimmer at a distance in the engines in many places. The men, women, children, country and houses are all black. . . . The country is very desolate every where; there are coals about, and the grass is quite blasted and black. I just now see an extraordinary building flaming with fire. The country continues black, engines flaming, coals, in abundance, every where, smoking and burning coal heaps, intermingled with wretched huts and carts and little ragged children.[22]

In Wales they visited Anglesey, '*dear* Plas Newydd', Caernarvon and Powis Castle. The tour also included three days with the Duke of Devonshire at Chatsworth, and luncheon 'on splendid gold plate' with Lord Shrewsbury at Alton Towers. At Oxford they saw the Sheldonian Theatre and the Bodleian Library, where Princess Victoria was shown Queen Elizabeth's Latin exercise book – 'when she was of my age (13)'. The journey ended with their return to Kensington Palace on 9 November.

King William IV was furious, suspecting that the Duchess and Conroy were endeavouring to set up a rival court: the late Duke of Kent had made no secret of his radical sympathies. Distracted by the worries of the Great Reform Bill going through Parliament that year, the publicly impartial but privately Tory King suspected that much harm could be done to the crown. He became 'so indecent in his wrath' that those around him feared for his sanity. When the Duchess of Kent and Princess Victoria visited the Isle of Wight in the summer of 1833, he was so angered by the 'continual popping in the shape of salutes' to his sister-in-law and niece that he ordered that in future the Royal Standard should be saluted only when the King or Queen was on board.

Now into her teens, the Princess's education expanded accordingly. Her tutor filled the whole morning with lessons, including more history and natural philosophy. Science lessons included lectures on alchemy and anatomy, the latter of which she found 'very disagreeable'.

Her adolescence coincided with a gradual liberalization in outlook towards children's literature. With the influence of the Romantic movement in the fine arts, classical influences were being replaced by those of German and Nordic culture. Modern fairy tales, particularly those of the Brothers Grimm, first published in English translation in 1823, were becoming more respectable. While the old-fashioned might deride them as unsuitable, largely on the grounds that their sense of fantasy might prove frightening, the old arguments about their being immoral or contrary to reason had lapsed. The historical novel and adventure story both came into their own, particularly with the books of Walter Scott. Popularly regarded as the 'American Scott' was James Fenimore Cooper, whose *Last of the Mohicans* was reportedly the first novel the Princess read. She found it 'very interesting' and 'very horrible'. Cooper's tales of the conflict of wild and civilized races, Indians and whites, still had enough underlying moral tone, but as robust adventure stories they were at the same time more appealing to the young mind, and the occasional 'very horrible' element surely served some purpose in preparing children for adult life.

Scott's novels were written mainly for an adult readership. The first British adventure stories written specially for children were Captain Marryat's *Peter Simple* (published in 1834) and *Mr Midshipman Easy* (1836). In a sense they still fulfilled a didactic purpose, with their patriotic appeal in praise of the Navy and the seafaring life, but as adventure stories they appealed greatly to boys.

The Princess also studied the great poets, especially Pope, Gray, Cowper, Goldsmith, 'parts of' Virgil in Latin, and Sir Walter Scott, the latter being the only one she really enjoyed. The magical simplicity of Maria Edgeworth's *Popular Tales* pleased her more than 'many a novel'.

Opera and ballet interested her increasingly. Her idol was Giulia Grisi, one of the foremost young opera singers of her day, and she was thrilled when Grisi came to Kensington Palace to sing on her sixteenth birthday. By this time, she had put her dolls away. Her circle of acquaintances was slowly increasing. At a ball given by King William on her fourteenth birthday, at St James's Palace, she had opened the dancing with her cousin, Prince George of Cambridge. He was only two months older than her, and his parents hoped that they might soon be betrothed.

When they returned home, she found consolation in the company of pets. The one thing Conroy did for which she was grateful was to give the Duchess of Kent a King Charles spaniel, Dash, whom the Princess adored, adopted and enjoyed dressing up in scarlet jacket and blue trousers. Dash evidently had a peaceful disposition and put up no resistance to being treated like a four-legged doll. That Christmas she gave him his own presents, three india-rubber balls, and two bits of gingerbread decorated with holly and candles. Whenever she was ill he spent 'his little life' in her room with her. In addition she had a horse called Rosa, who like Dash accompanied her on the progresses. Caged birds also lived in the royal quarters at Kensington, in particular a tame old canary which came out of its cage to peck gently at Dash's fur, and a parakeet which laughed and coughed in faithful imitation of the grown-ups.

The year of 1835 was to prove a decisive one in the Princess's childhood. On 30 July she was confirmed at the Chapel Royal, St James's. The day before, the Duchess of Kent had given her three books to prepare her for the step, two of which she had read by the following day. 'I felt that my confirmation was one of the most solemn and important events and acts in my life;' she wrote, 'and that I trusted it might have a salutary effect on my mind.'[23] It was overshadowed when the King counted the Duchess of Kent's retinue, declared it was too large and ordered Conroy out of the chapel. The comptroller bitterly resented this public indignity and never forgave the King. A power struggle was going on at Kensington, and the Princess was aware of efforts to dismiss the faithful Lehzen. 'I was very much affected indeed when she came home,' she wrote in her journal, evidently not just through religious awe, but also overcome by misery at the thought of her security being taken from her.

A month later the royal progresses began again with a grand tour of the north. The Princess looked forward to them with scant enthusiasm. The 'Kensington system' was preying on her emotions; she knew the effort of travelling would make her ill, and that the King would be upset. The Duchess and Conroy brushed her objections aside impatiently, and on 3 September 1835, in heat and dust, suffering from headache and backache, Princess Victoria set out for Yorkshire, taking in the York Musical Festival, Doncaster races, and the Belvoir mausoleum. Her health had not improved, and by the time they reached Holkham, she was so exhausted she nearly fell asleep over dinner.

At the end of September they moved to Ramsgate for an autumn holiday. The Princess's spirits rose, for King Leopold of the Belgians was coming to stay for a few days. She had not seen him for several years, and had never met his wife, Queen Louise, daughter of Louis-Philippe, King of the French. Only seven years separated the Queen Consort and the future Queen regnant, and Louise immediately put her niece at ease, telling her to treat her as an elder sister. Victoria had a delightful time trying on her aunt's Parisian clothes while King Leopold, as yet unaware of the darker aspects of the 'Kensington system', went for a long walk with Conroy, assuring him that with tact, he might still win himself 'a very good position'.

Two days before the King and Queen were due to depart, Princess Victoria awoke feeling sick. By the time they left, she was too ill and wretched to eat. Her physician Dr James Clark, appointed to the Duchess of Kent's household the previous year, examined her and thought it was 'a slight indisposition' which would pass in two or three days. Lehzen was concerned that it was more than that, but the Duchess told her that she and the Princess were exaggerating. In fact, the illness worsened, and the Princess was confined in her room for five weeks. Whether it was typhoid, tonsilitis, or collapse from strain, has never been ascertained.

Although ill, the Princess was a fighter – as she needed to be. Backed up by the Duchess, Conroy strode into her room one day carrying a pencil and paper which he asked the sixteen-year-old invalid to sign. It was a pledge by which she would agree to appoint him as her private secretary on her succession to the throne. Fortunately Lehzen was in the room as well, and despite his fiery temper, Conroy was forced to leave the room, muttering angrily, without the signature.

The Princess had recovered by January 1836 and they returned to Kensington Palace. Four months later, a few days before her seventeenth birthday, her Coburg cousins, Ernest and Albert, were invited to come and stay. She was very taken with them, 'particularly Albert, who is the most reflective of the two', and she felt wretched when they returned home.

In August King William IV celebrated his seventy-first birthday. The Duchess of Kent had declined to attend Queen Adelaide's birthday on 13 August, but she could not refuse the royal command to attend that of the King the following week. Enraged by the Duchess's appropriation of a suite of rooms at Kensington Palace, he made a rambling speech at the end of the dinner in which he trusted that his life would be spared for nine months longer, in order that no regency would take place; 'I should then have the satisfaction of leaving the royal authority to the personal exercise of that young lady (pointing to the Princess), the heiress presumptive of the Crown, and not in the hands of a person now near me, who is surrounded by evil advisers and who is herself incompetent to act with propriety in the station in which she would be placed.'[24]

Princess Victoria burst into tears. The Duchess of Kent ordered her carriage forthwith, and was only prevailed upon to remain another day with great difficulty.

Over Christmas 1836, which was spent at Claremont, the Princess became greatly fascinated by a gypsy encampment nearby – in her words, 'the chief ornament of the Portsmouth Road.'[25] She longed to do something for these poor yet proud, cheerful people. The contrast between their affection for each other and her own unhappiness at home was painful, and she was frustrated when her efforts to help were mocked. She and Lehzen both read the Revd George Crabbe's *Gipsies' Advocate*, and were convinced that poor folk would respond to kindness; one should not be ashamed to speak to them. It was a view which apparently found no favour with Conroy, presumably because he objected to the idea of Princess Victoria thinking for herself in this manner. Such lack of prejudice was not only fitting in a future Queen, it was characteristic of the only child of a royal Duke who had been regarded with suspicion by most of his brothers for his liberal, if not left-wing, views. Nevertheless, she persuaded the Duchess of Kent to send them soup and blankets.

It is rather touching to read from her journal that on Christmas Day, she and Lehzen visited them in the afternoon, particularly to enquire after the health of one of the women who had had a baby nine days previously. She longed to ask them to call the child Leopold, after her uncle King Leopold, on whose birthday the child had been born, but instead the baby was named Francis. 'I cannot say how happy I am that these poor creatures are assisted,' she wrote, 'for they are such a nice set of Gipsies, so quiet, so affectionate to one another, so discreet, not at all forward or importunate, and *so* grateful; so unlike the gossiping, fortune-telling race gipsies . . . I shall go to bed happy, knowing they are better off and more comfortable.'[26]

In February 1837 the Princess saw a train for the first time: 'We went to see the Railroad near Hersham, & saw the steam carriage pass with surprising quickness, striking sparks as it flew along the railroad, enveloped in clouds of smoke & making a loud noise. It is a curious thing indeed!'[27]

No less curious, perhaps, was the outcome of the power struggle at Kensington. King William had publicly expressed, albeit in somewhat embarrassing terms, his intention of living to see his niece and heir celebrate her eighteenth birthday, and thus be spared a regency under the Duchess of Kent and 'King' John Conroy. His wish was granted. He offered her a grant of £10,000 a year entirely free of her mother's control, an independent Keeper of her Privy Purse, and the right to appoint her own ladies-in-waiting. Although the letter was delivered personally to her (after the Duchess and Conroy had attempted to intercept the messenger), she was forced to decline the offer. As the King knew only too well, 'Victoria has not written that letter'.[28] Yet she did not have long to wait. On 19 June 1837 it was evident that the King had only a few hours left, and at six o'clock the following morning, the Archbishop of Canterbury and the King's Lord Chamberlain, Lord Conyngham, drove to Kensington Palace, demanding to see 'the Queen'.

Awakened by her mother, 'I got out of bed and went into my sitting-room (only in my dressing-gown) and *alone*, and saw them,' she noted in her journal. They told her that the King had died shortly after 2 a.m., 'and consequently that I am *Queen*'.[29]

2

'Mamma d'une nombreuse famille'

Queen Victoria and Prince Albert of Saxe-Coburg Gotha were married at the Chapel Royal, St James's, on 10 February 1840. Early the following morning, the diarist Charles Greville noticed them walking in the park. He thought it 'strange that a bridal night should be so short', and concluded that this was no way to provide the country with a Prince of Wales.

Until they had children, the heir was her uncle Ernest Augustus, Duke of Cumberland and, since the death of King William IV, King of Hanover. Although he proved himself a capable ruler, he was the most unpopular member of the royal family as far as the British public was concerned. He was credited (quite unjustly) with various crimes, including incest with one of his sisters and the murder of his valet, and the Whig government detested his ultra-Tory politics, which they had considered an adverse influence on the last two Kings.

Greville and the rest of her subjects need not have worried. The Queen hated and dreaded the idea of childbearing, and wanted at least a year of 'happy enjoyment' with Albert before any children came along to disturb their tranquillity. Nevertheless, within a few weeks she was *enceinte*. Her confinement was expected in December, but she went into labour three weeks early. On 21 November 1840, at ten minutes to two in the afternoon, her first child, a daughter, was born at Buckingham Palace.

The Queen had expressed an objection to having large numbers of people present at the birth to attend as witnesses. Only Dr Locock, the nurse Mrs Lilly, and Prince Albert himself, were present. In the next room were several Cabinet ministers, including the Prime Minister Lord Melbourne, Palmerston, and

Lord John Russell, the Archbishop of Canterbury, the Bishop of London, and Lord Erroll, Lord Steward of the Household. They heard Dr Locock's voice through the open door; 'Oh, Madam, it is a Princess.' 'Never mind, the next will be a Prince,' the Queen declared. The baby was wrapped in flannel, taken into the room and laid upon a specially prepared table for their inspection, then returned to her room to be dressed.

'A perfect little child was born,' the Queen wrote, 'but alas a girl and not a boy, as we both had so hoped and wished for. We were, I am afraid, sadly disappointed.'[1] This disappointment was shortlived. Almost twenty years later, on the birth of her first granddaughter, she would write to the mother (this newly born daughter) that girls were 'much more amusing'.

All the Queen's children were born at home, either at Buckingham Palace or Windsor Castle. The same nurse, Mrs Lilly, assisted her during all nine confinements, and Prince Albert remained by her side most of the time to carry, comfort and assist her, to read and sing, or summarize despatches and deal with visitors throughout the two weeks or so following the birth while she remained in bed.

As the birth had not been expected until early December, the wet-nurse – Mrs Southey, sister-in-law of the poet – was still at home in the Isle of Wight. A page was sent for her, and brought her over in an open boat from Cowes to Southampton, so she arrived at the Palace by 2 a.m. the following day. The Queen's dressing-room was fitted up as a temporary nursery, until apartments were ready for the Princess. Among the fittings were a marble and a silver bath, and a cradle in the form of a nautilus.

Before the end of the Queen's 'lying-in', another child – this time uninvited – was in the Palace. About ten days after the birth, Mrs Lilly was woken shortly after 1 a.m. by a noise in the Queen's sitting-room. She called a page, Kinnaird, to help her investigate. Kinnaird looked under the Queen's sofa, and hurriedly backed away without saying anything. Meanwhile the ever-faithful Baroness Lehzen had appeared. She pushed the sofa aside, to reveal a boy curled up on the floor. He was recognized as 'the boy Jones', who had paid a similar clandestine visit to the Palace two years previously. Proudly, he claimed that he could get over the wall on Constitution Hill and creep through one of the windows.

When asked why he entered Her Majesty's apartment, he said that he wanted to know 'how they lived at the Palace'. He had no weapons or stolen property, but boasted that he had sat on the throne, 'that he saw the Queen and heard the Princess Royal squall'. He had slept under one of the servants' beds, and helped himself to food from the kitchens.

Home Office officials established that he was Edmund Jones, the son of a Westminster tailor. Aged seventeen, he was stunted in growth and looked very young for his age. He was sent to a House of Correction in Tothill Street as a rogue and vagabond for three months, and put to work on the treadmill. Undaunted, he paid another such visit after his release in March the following year, and after a similar punishment he was sent to sea.

Meanwhile the Queen and her daughter throve. The Queen sat up for the first time since the birth on 6 December and got out of bed again the following day. On 19 January 1841 the hereditary style and distinction of Princess Royal was conferred on the new Princess. The previous holder of the style, Charlotte, Queen of Württemberg, had died in 1828.

Three weeks later, on the Queen's first wedding anniversary, the Princess was christened in the throne room at Buckingham Palace. She was given the names Victoria Adelaide Mary Louisa, the second after the Queen Dowager, the third and fourth in honour of the Duchess of Kent, both of whom were among the sponsors. The others were the Queen's aunt Mary, Duchess of Gloucester, her uncles the Duke of Sussex, Leopold, King of the Belgians, and Albert's father, the Duke of Saxe-Coburg Gotha. The latter was so offended by Albert's refusal to demand a personal allowance for him and his dissipated lifestyle from the Queen that he did not even answer an invitation to attend the ceremony. In his absence, the Duke of Wellington was asked to stand proxy for him.

Also present was Lord Melbourne, who remarked about the Princess, 'How she looked about her, quite conscious that the stir was all about herself. This is the time the character is formed!'[2]

A new font was used, made of silver gilt in the shape of a water lily supporting a large shell. Inside the rim of the small shell were water lilies floating around the edge, and water was brought specially from the river Jordan.

'The Christening went off very well,' Prince Albert wrote to the Dowager Duchess of Saxe-Gotha Altenburg. 'Your little great-grandchild behaved with great propriety, and like a Christian. She was awake, but did not cry at all, and seemed to crow with immense satisfaction at the lights and brilliant uniforms, for she is very intelligent and observing.'[3]

Although this daughter was the first of nine children, Queen Victoria was not particularly maternal by nature. Until a baby was six months old, she thought it 'froglike' and ugly. The very idea of childbirth revolted her; to her it was 'the shadow-side of marriage', or *die Schattenseite*, an indelicate subject which sounded less repulsive in a different language. According to Elizabeth Longford, memories of the Flora Hastings affair* may have accounted for 'her almost Jansenist disgust for the things of the body, which combined strangely with her healthy Hanoverian nature.'[4]

The Queen firmly refused to breast-feed her children. Prince Albert begged her to, and the Duchess of Kent, who had given her daughter 'maternal nourishment' supported his argument, but she would not be swayed. It has been suggested that her main influence in the matter was that of Lehzen, who told her of the old wives' tale prevalent in Germany that hereditary taints were passed on through the mother's milk.[5] Breast-feeding was considered unusual for a lady at the time of the Queen's accession, but by the 1840s manuals on childcare were recommending the practice, and it became popular among the aristocracy.

King Leopold had correctly predicted that the Princess Royal would be the first of several children in the royal nurseries, and told his niece so. She did not welcome the prospect:

I think, dearest Uncle, you cannot *really* wish me to be the 'Mamma d'une *nombreuse* famille,' for I think you will see

---

*Lady Flora Hastings was a spinster lady-in-waiting of the Duchess of Kent, a close friend of Conroy and bitter enemy of Lehzen. In 1839 the Queen suspected that she had become pregnant by Conroy and cold-shouldered her. A medical examination proved that she was a virgin, and that the swelling in her stomach was caused by cancer. She died a few months later, but not before her family had made considerable capital out of the incident, and the Queen's popularity had plummeted accordingly.

with me the great inconvenience a *large* family would be to us all, and particularly to the country, independent of the hardship and inconvenience to myself; men never think, at least seldom think, what a hard task it is for us women to go through this *very often*.[6]

To her sometimes ill-concealed fury the Queen discovered, about the time of the christening, that she was 'in for it' again. Her first pregnancy had been comparatively easy, but the summer of 1841 was a difficult one, not least because of the fall of the government and the resignation of her beloved mentor Lord Melbourne. His successor, Robert Peel, was particularly admired by Prince Albert – who was at pains to keep the crown above party politics – but at first the Queen treated him with hostility.

Prince Albert was very protective of his daughter, or 'Pussy' as her parents affectionately called her for the first few years of her life. Before her birth he had asked Queen Adelaide why her little girls had died in infancy. The Queen Dowager told him that they had been weak from the start, slow to gain weight, and uninterested in their food. He watched cautiously for similar signs in the Princess Royal, and was relieved that she appeared to thrive at first. He was equally apprehensive that she might be killed in a carriage accident. Having seen a young Coburg cousin killed by a bolting horse, and mindful of the bad state of English roads, his fear of accidents bordered on the obsessive. When the court went to Windsor for Christmas, he held his month-old baby in his arms himself, warning the coachman repeatedly to watch out for ice or pot-holes on the journey.

He adored his daughter and visited her several times in the day, oblivious to stony looks from the nurses and gentle teasing from the Queen. 'I think you would be amused to see Albert dancing her in his arms,' she wrote to King Leopold (5 January 1841); 'he makes a capital nurse (which I do not, and she is much too heavy for me to carry), and she always seems so happy to go with him.'[7]

The inner circle at court who saw the Princess Royal could testify that she was thriving. Outside, people were less certain. The Queen's Lady of the Bedchamber, Sarah, Lady Lyttelton, was alarmed at (and partly convinced by) the spate of rumours sweeping London – that the baby heir to the throne was blind, deaf, dumb, an imbecile, or deformed. As nobody outside the family and household ever saw her, public imagination was bound to run riot. Not until she strolled through the grounds of Windsor Castle one summer day did she come across a baby being taken out in her pram. The little blue-eyed girl, 'absurdly like the Queen', was evidently a fine child in every way. Lady Lyttelton suggested that she should be seen by the public. She was therefore taken for regular rides in the carriage, clapping her tiny hands and chuckling as the crowds pressed close, captivated by the chubby figure in white muslin dress and Quaker bonnet. Lady Lyttelton remarked with amusement that before long she would have seen every pair of teeth in the kingdom.

Unfortunately, after a few months the Princess was not so well. By late summer she was unable to digest her food, lost weight, cut her teeth with difficulty, and cried a great deal. The blame was largely laid at the door of Mrs Southey, a hypochondriac who was rather too fond of cheese and beer. Dr Clark's remedy for the baby was 'soothing medicine', a solution containing laudanum, which made her pale and lethargic.

At that time drugs, medicines and restoratives were prescribed for children to an extent which seems to have bordered on the reckless. Doctors frequently recommended wine, and nurses were liberal in making their young charges take pills or powder, a dose of brimstone and treacle, castor oil, liquorice, or a spoonful of Godfrey's cordial. The latter was a mixture of laudanum and syrup, easily purchased from any chemist over the counter, and an effective tranquillizer, reducing children to stupefaction for hours on end. Sometimes the hours were, literally, endless. According to a report of 1844, 'great numbers of children perish, either suddenly from an overdose, or, as more commonly happens, slowly, painfully and insidiously.'[8] A few households had the sense to ban 'Godfrey's cordial', but less wisely mixed large quantities of gin with their children's milk.

The Queen's second pregnancy was more difficult than her first, and her state of depression was exacerbated by Pussy's problems. 'Till the end of August she was such a magnificent, strong fat child,' she noted with concern, 'that it is a great grief to see her so thin, pale and changed.'[9] Dr Clark suggested various changes to her diet to make her put on weight; asses' milk and chicken broth, cream in her cereal, and butter on her rusks, were all tried. The resulting mixture was so rich for her that she became more sick than ever, and still lost weight.

By this time the Queen's confinement was approaching. Twice during October the doctors thought she might give birth prematurely. On 9 November, at 10.50 p.m., 'a fine large boy' was born. The Queen admitted in her journal (2 December) that 'my sufferings were really very severe, and I don't know what I should have done, but for the great comfort and support my beloved Albert was to me.'[10] Pussy was 'terrified & not at all pleased with her little brother'.[11]

The new heir to the throne was created Prince of Wales on 4 December 1841, and christened Albert Edward in St George's Chapel, Windsor, on 25 January 1842. Handel's *Hallelujah Chorus* was played on the organ, and the Duke of Wellington carried the Sword of State. Lord Melbourne, writing on 1 December, approved the choice of his maternal grandfather's name; '*Edward* is a good English appellation, and has a certain degree of popularity attached to it from ancient recollections.'[12]

The Queen was delighted with her eldest son; 'our little boy is a wonderfully strong and large child, with very large dark blue eyes, a finely formed but somewhat large nose, and a pretty little mouth; I *hope* and *pray* he may be like his dearest Papa.'[13] From the first, he enjoyed perfect health and 'crowing spirits', with none of his sister's digestive problems.

Prince Albert was sure that slackness and ignorance among the nursery staff were almost entirely responsible for his daughter's ill-health; and Lehzen, he maintained, was the chief culprit. He resented her for her possessive attitude towards the Queen, and though no admirer of the Conroy, who had long since been 'persuaded to retire', never forgave her for coming between the Queen and the Duchess of Kent, who had long since become reconciled. He had no faith either in Dr Clark, who he knew only told the Queen what she wanted to hear and – Albert suspected – supplemented his salary with secret payments from the firms which supplied the expensive medicines and diets he prescribed. Baron Christian von Stockmar, a physician from Coburg who also served as confidential adviser and father figure to the sovereign and her husband, had warned them of Clark's incompetence.

The room was kept too hot because Mrs Southey, the Lady Superintendent, was anaemic, suffered from poor circulation, and would accept no contradiction from Mrs Roberts, the more enlightened nurse. Lehzen had no official place in the nursery, although her friendship with Queen Victoria allowed her to do virtually as she pleased. Albert frequently found her there, holding Pussy in her arms and breathing caraway seeds over her, gossiping with Mrs Southey who sat wrapped in shawls, warming her feet in front of a roaring fire, with all the windows shut. This was contrary to the recommendations of Stockmar, who had insisted that temperatures in the nursery should be kept down in order to discourage germs and sickness.

Lehzen had an ardent defender in King Leopold, who had tried to get her naturalized as a British subject so she could attend Privy Council meetings and become the Queen's public adviser, an ill-considered plan only thwarted by Stockmar's intervention. Stockmar could see all too clearly that Lehzen was outstaying her welcome and coming between husband and wife. He and Lord Melbourne both advised Albert in August 1841 to use the change of government as an excuse for demanding her resignation, but Albert did not have the heart to do so, partly as he feared an 'exciting scene' from his heavily pregnant wife, and partly as King Leopold was staying at Windsor at the time.

Shortly after Christmas, Albert took the Queen to Claremont for a few days. She was suffering from post-natal depression and needed a change of scene. They were recalled to Buckingham Palace in mid-January by an urgent message from Stockmar: Pussy was worse. Her parents rushed up to the nursery to see her, and found her looking very thin and white.

Albert dreaded the worst. Was his daughter fatally stricken with consumption, or some similar illness? A difference of opinion between him and Mrs Roberts made the Queen lose her temper. She snapped at him, defending the nurse and telling her husband that he wanted to drive her out of the nursery while he as good as murdered their child. He turned ashen with horror, shouted, 'I must have patience!' and walked out of the room, slamming the door. Later there was a violent row between husband and wife, which ended in the distraught Queen telling him angrily that she wished she had never married him.

Verbal communication being impossible, Albert retired to his study to regain his composure, then picked up his pen and wrote the Queen a message telling her bluntly that Dr Clark had 'mismanaged' their daughter and poisoned her with calomel, and her mother had starved her; 'I shall have nothing more to do with it; take the child away and do as you like and if she dies you will have it on your conscience.'[14]

In desperation the Queen turned towards Stockmar, acting as devil's advocate. She begged him to tell Lehzen that there had been 'a little misunderstanding'. Albert saw that the time had come to resolve the festering situation once and for all. Lehzen, he told Stockmar in terms which were positively vitriolic for one of his restrained nature, was 'a crazy, common, stupid intriguer, obsessed with lust of power, who regards herself as a demi-god, and anyone who refuses to acknowledge her as such, as a criminal.'[15] The Queen, he went on, was a fine character 'but warped in many respects by wrong upbringing'.

Written messages continued between husband and wife, whose tempers were at such a pitch that they dared not see each other for a few days, with Stockmar acting as peace envoy. At length the Queen gave in. The nursery management should be reformed, she agreed, and Lehzen – with whom, the Queen admitted, she discussed very little now – was to be given her notice.

In July Albert told the Queen that the Baroness wished to leave in two months' time and retire for the sake of her health. Accepting a pension, much of which she spent on establishing her brothers' children in careers, she slipped away in September without saying goodbye, so as not to cause a scene, and settled with her sister in Bückeburg. Queen and Baroness continued to correspond regularly, and the Queen met her briefly on subsequent visits to Germany.*

Mrs Southey left the royal nursery soon afterwards by mutual agreement. On 26 December 1841 she offered her resignation to take effect as soon as somebody else could be found. She did not feel 'equal' to her duties, was frequently homesick and wanted more time to visit her friends. The Queen and Albert agreed

*Baroness Lehzen died in 1870, aged eighty-six.

that she had been plainly inadequate, and were not sorry to see her go.

In March 1842 the Queen complained to Lord Melbourne that the children were being left to 'low people', and surrounded by a quarrelsome atmosphere. Melbourne agreed that a lady of high rank would be more suitable: she would have greater authority, and be less likely to have her head turned by such a position than somebody from the middle class. The following month Lady Lyttelton was appointed as new governess, in charge of the royal nursery. Born Lady Sarah Spencer, she had married William Henry Lyttelton in March 1813. He succeeded to the title of Baron Lyttelton in 1828, and died in 1837, leaving her with five children. The following year she became Lady of the Bedchamber to Queen Victoria.

Old-fashioned in dress and outlook, she was very tolerant of and patient with children. She did not believe in punishments, on the grounds that 'one is never *sure* they are fully understood by the child as belonging to the naughtiness'.[16] The Queen disapproved of her High Church views, and would never permit discussion of ecclesiastical subjects; and Lady Lyttelton's views on Albert's games of chess on Sundays tended towards the Puritanical. Otherwise there were no major disagreements between the royal employers and their new employee.

Her first encounter with the children was not encouraging. At first sight of her, Pussy screamed so loudly, that nothing would pacify her short of Lady Lyttelton leaving the room. Though the little girl remained 'very grave and distant' towards her for a while, she soon rewarded the governess with her affection and respect, and the nickname 'Laddle'. Much of the trouble, Lady Lyttelton was convinced, was as a result of the Princess being 'over-watched and over-doctored'.

That the Princess Royal was a regular subject of attention gave the governess grounds for some irritation, as she noted in a letter written a few months after her appointment:

I wish there were no portraits being done of the Princess Royal, and that all her fattest and biggest and most forbidding looking relations, some with bald heads, some with great moustaches, some with black bushy eyebrows, some with staring, distorted, short-sighted eyes, did not always come to see her at once and make her naughty and her governess cross. Poor little body! She is always expected to be good, civil and sensible.[17]

Almost every visiting dignitary to Windsor Castle and Buckingham Palace had to come and admire this delightful child with fair curly hair and bright blue eyes, her parents being only too pleased to show her off. The Duke of Wellington, ever the courtier, pretended to treat her like an adult, bowing low and kissing her hand. Tsar Nicholas I of Russia, with his rolling eyes and loud, harsh laugh, fascinated her, and let her sit on his knee while she sucked a huge bloodstone hanging from his watch chain. She learnt to speak fluently very quickly, and distracted her doting mother when she was trying to concentrate on state papers. Ministers would find her crawling under their feet or pulling herself up on their trouser-legs.

The year 1842 was one of 'respite'. The Queen became pregnant later that summer, but was relieved that the year would pass without her having another child; and with Lehzen gone, personal relations improved rapidly. In later years she would tell her family that as babies her two eldest 'difficult' children caused her more trouble than the other seven put together. Child psychologists of the time, had they existed, would have certainly attributed the trouble to the power struggles in the nursery which were now thankfully over. With Lady Lyttelton in charge, and the motherly Mrs Sly in place of Mrs Roberts, who had barely been on speaking terms with Prince Albert, harmony reigned.

On 25 April 1843 the Queen had a second daughter, named Alice. The Princess Royal, she noted, was 'very tender with her little sister, who is a pretty and large baby and we think will be the beauty of the family'.[18] 'Fat Alice' was nicknamed Fatima by the parents. The Queen recovered rapidly, became bored with lying-in, and got up a few days later. Albert, the household noticed, spent less time playing the part of the adoring husband than formerly. At Christmas the previous year, he had not been so eager to push his wife's ice-chair round the frozen lake, had less time to spare for card games or charades in the evenings, and was impatient to get back to his study so he could catch up with working on state papers.

Nevertheless he could always make time to spend with his children. Like his wife, he had suffered from a lonely, difficult childhood. The younger of two boys, his early days had been scarred by the banishment of his adored mother for adultery, and the hurtful sarcasm of his even less faithful father. The elder son, Ernest, was a happy-go-lucky young man who had much in common with his namesake father, not least a taste for dissipation and the morals of an alley cat. With his introspective nature, Albert bore the psychological scars for life. Later he told his eldest daughter that he 'could not bear to think of his childhood, he had been so unhappy and miserable, and had many a time wished himself out of this world'.[19]

As a father, he intended to give his sons and daughters the happy childhood that he had never known. He was affectionate, patient and understanding with the children, ever ready to enter the nursery and play with the youngsters. He loved to dandle one on each knee while he played the organ, or teach them to sing nursery rhymes. Queen Victoria was the first to admit that she was never completely at ease with children, be they hers or anybody else's. Albert it was who never had to be persuaded to play hide-and-seek, turn somersaults, chase butterflies, demonstrate card games, perform magic tricks, or fly kites with the growing family.

Every Easter he helped to organize a hunt for eggs. It had been the custom in Germany for fathers to hide coloured eggs on Maundy Thursday and send his children to find them. They were boiled hard and quite inedible, but it was a game of which generations of royal children never tired.

Prince Albert's eager encouragement of them in their nursery games reveals him to have been far from the cold, remote *paterfamilias*, whose children were terrified of him, of popular legend. In the nursery at Claremont, he enjoyed building houses with Vicky's wooden bricks, so tall that he had to stand on a chair to finish them, reaching above his head. 'Such a fall as it made! He enjoyed it much the most.'[20] When they were older he would take them to see the waxworks at Madame Tussaud's, or the animals at London Zoo, like generations of proud fathers ever since who enjoyed mixing education with pleasure.

His regular nursery visits gave him the chance to prepare special surprises. When Princess Alice was only a few days old, he smuggled the painter Edwin Landseer in, to paint her in her cradle, guarded by Dandie, the black terrier. The result was ready, framed and wreathed with flowers for the Queen's birthday the following month.

Princess Alice was generally a placid baby, although Lady Lyttelton recorded one exception to this rule when she was ten months old – at her vaccination taken 'from a *magnificent* baby. Such a duett [*sic*] of shrieks as the two kept up, staring and terrified at each other, and ascribing the cuts, no doubt, to each other, instead of Mr Brown [the doctor]!'[21]

There were regular outbursts between the two elder children. Some sibling rivalry between the Princess Royal and the Prince of Wales was inevitable. Fights in their mother's room early in the morning were nothing unusual, and sending them downstairs separately did not stop the Princess from picking quarrels with him as soon as they were together again.

Both were jealous of the other; Pussy had screamed and refused to be pacified when taken for her first peep at the small occupant of the cradle that had formerly been hers. 'The Boy' was slow to cut his teeth, learn to walk and talk. His sister, so much more forward in every way, could not resist teasing him. Overshadowed by her intelligence and obvious cleverness, and not slow to notice how she was petted and admired by their parents and vistors at court, he fought back the only way he knew how, with fists and displays of temper.

Noticing that he seemed to sense his inadequacy beside his elder sister, Lady Lyttelton was quick to spring to his defence. In February 1844 she found him

not articulate like his sister, but rather babyish in accent . . . altogether backward in language, very intelligent, and generous and good-tempered, with a few passions and *stampings* occasionally; most exemplary in politeness and manner, bows and offers his hand beautifully, besides saluting *à la militaire* – all unbidden. He is very handsome, but still very small every way.[22]

In her sympathy, she underestimated the 'passions'. Shortly after his second birthday, Dr Clark detected the cause of his lateness in talking with any clarity – a minor speech impediment. This, and a slight stutter (which he soon outgrew), prevented him from making himself understood properly. The impediment remained, and was the cause of his guttural accent. Contrary to popular belief, the future King Edward VII did not speak English with a pronounced German accent, although his voice had a deep guttural tone, with a German style of speech and particular stress on certain syllables. The children spoke nothing but English at home, and as they generally saw more of their nurses and governesses than their father – the only one in their childhood circle with a definite German accent – Prince Albert Edward did not acquire a German intonation. Warned of the problem, Albert treated his son's mild handicap with patience and commonsense, and there was a rapid improvement.

Between Bertie and Alice there was an exceptionally close bond, which remained so until death separated them. When the latter was only eighteen months old, the Queen remarked on their being 'the greatest friends & always playing together'.[23] Alice could bring out the best in him, and on the rare occasions that she was sent to her room for being naughty, he would creep silently up the stairs and along the corridors, only to be intercepted by a watchful adult and confess guiltily that he was 'going to give Alee a morsel of news'.

On 6 August 1844 the Queen gave birth to a second son. Describing his wife's confinement, Albert wrote to his brother Ernest, who had succeeded their father as Duke of Saxe-Coburg Gotha six months previously, that 'she let us wait a long time and consequently the child is unusually large and strong'.[24]

The new Prince was christened on 6 September, and given the names Alfred Ernest Albert. To the family he was always 'Affie'. His sponsors at the ceremony were his aunt Alexandrine, Duchess of Saxe-Coburg Gotha (represented *in absentia* by the Duchess of Kent), Prince George of Cambridge, and Prince William of Prussia.

Affie inherited the full measure of Hanoverian high spirits. He appeared completely oblivious of danger; as soon as he could walk on his own, he climbed out of windows and balanced on ledges thirty feet or more above the ground unless restrained, or jumped across fast-running streams before he could swim. He slid down banisters, falling off and concussing himself, once narrowly avoiding a fractured skull. Despite a severe scolding he would do the same the next day. If sent to his room or given a sharp smack by his mother for fooling about, he would be duly penitent – and do just the same the next day. Almost every week he had some minor accident, but emerged unscathed apart from bruises or the occasional black eye.

In the spring of 1845, when Affie was nine months old, Mrs Sly resigned, and her place was taken by Mary Ann Thurston. A young widow of thirty-five, her husband had died before their first wedding anniversary and two months before the birth of their daughter Elizabeth, or 'Libbie'. Mrs Thurston soon fitted into her new role, second only to Lady Lyttelton in the nursery hierarchy, and it was only a matter of months before Queen Victoria was praising her 'way with the children'.

'It gives me the greatest pleasure to be able to announce to Your Majesty that yesterday afternoon at 3 o'clock the Queen was safely delivered of a Princess,' Prince Albert wrote to King Frederick William IV of Prussia (26 May 1846). 'The many proofs of friendship which Your Majesty has given to us assure me that you will receive the news of this gladdening event with your former interest.'[25]

To his brother Ernest, he wrote the same day that 'Heaven gave us a third little daughter. She came into this world rather blue; but she is quite well now. Victoria suffered longer and more than the other times and she will have to remain very quiet to recover from all.'[26] Though it was a severe and protracted labour, mother and child both made a quick recovery, and the latter grew up to be physically the toughest of the royal sisters.

She was christened on 25 July at Buckingham Palace, and given the names Helena Augusta Victoria. Two of her sponsors were present in person, the Hereditary Grand Duke of Mecklenburg-Strelitz, and the Duchess of Cambridge; the third sponsor, the Duchess of Orleans, was represented by the infant's grandmother, the Duchess of Kent. Princess Helena disgraced herself by alternately crying lustily and sucking her thumb at the ceremony.

Lady Lyttelton left a description of Alice on her fourth birthday, 1847:

Dear Princess Alice is too pretty, in her low frock and pearl necklace, tripping about and blushing and smiling at her honours. The whole family, indeed, appear to advantage on birthdays; no tradesman or county squire can keep one with such hearty simple affection and enjoyment. *One* present I think we shall all wish to live farther off: a live lamb, all over pink ribbons and bells. He is already the greatest pet, as one may suppose.

Princess Alice's pet lamb is the cause of many tears. He will not take to his mistress, but runs away lustily, and will soon butt at her, though she is most coaxy, and said to him in her sweetest tones, after kissing his nose often, 'Milly, *dear* Milly! *do* you like me?'[27]

Vicky and Alice were always close. They shared a bedroom, each others clothes, and general confidences. Like Bertie, perhaps Alice was discouraged at being apparently put in the shade by their brilliant, clever eldest sister and looking slow by comparison. Yet she was intelligent and quick to learn, not given to showing off, and more tactful. A former dresser of the Queen, who was unusually tall, passed the royal children playing in the corridor. The Prince of Wales made a joke about her height, but Alice retorted loudly and clearly, 'It is very nice to be tall; Papa would like us all to be tall.'[28]

Vicky took on the mantle of elder sister-protector, and sometimes this led to pranks. Aged seven, Vicky was in an obstreperous mood one day after an argument with Lady Lyttelton. Walking out of the palace nursery in a sulk, she invited Alice to come exploring with her into some of the rooms they were not generally allowed to visit. When they found a servant girl cleaning the fireplace, Vicky promptly announced that they would help. The girl felt she could hardly say anything, even when the Princesses stopped working on the grate and applied the brushes to her face and clothes. They scampered away, leaving the unfortunate employee to pluck up courage to go and tidy herself up before anybody else saw her. On her way she had to walk past an amazed Prince Albert, who insisted on knowing what had happened. Within minutes a stony-faced Queen Victoria, leading a daughter firmly by each hand, marched across the courtyard to the servants' quarters. The girl, now clean again, was called and each Princess begged her pardon. Later they were sent out by carriage to go shopping – to buy a new dress, cap and apron from their pocket money.

There was no question of the royal children being given unlimited amounts of money to indulge their every whim. Queen Victoria had known what it was like to scrimp and save. Her promise to pay off the outstanding debts left by her spendthrift father as soon as she was in a position to do so had left her with a horror of extravagance. Stockmar had never ceased to impress on her and Prince Albert how the free and easy ways of King George IV had damaged the monarchy's standing at a time of national economic crisis. The Coburgs had had a reputation for parsimony, and Prince Albert proved himself adept at financial management. His reorganization of the royal household had been done partly with a view to cutting back unnecessary expenditure, and in some cases servants' wages, a move which did not endear him to everyone. *Punch*, founded in 1841 and frequently critical of royalty in its early years, rumoured that he dabbled in railway shares, and when he won prizes at agricultural shows for animals and produce from the Windsor farms, other competitors were disgusted to watch him pocket the silver coins he received as prize money.

To some Prince Albert appeared mean, but he could never be accused of spending recklessly on the family while others went hungry. In Luton it was believed that the Queen was advocating having all children under the age of five put to death as famine was so severe. At Christmas 1842 he had suggested that they should set a good example to the nation by celebrating less lavishly than before. There were fewer courses and less wine at dinner, a mild sacrifice which could perhaps be partly – but not wholly – explained by his aversion to drunkenness and antipathy to rich food.

On 18 March 1848 a fifth daughter appeared. Princess Louise had the dubious distinction of being born during the year of revolutions. During the previous month the exiled French royal family had come to seek refuge in England, and Queen Victoria was allowed barely a moment's rest while approaching her sixth confinement, comforting her harassed, careworn husband one moment, helping to organize accommodation for their Bourbon guests the next. The baby, she was convinced, would be sure to turn out 'something peculiar'. Louise was perfectly healthy, and enjoyed excellent health until her death over ninety-one years later. In one sense, though, she would turn out 'something peculiar'. As a grown woman she would prove to be the rebel of the family.

Queen Victoria lacked the maternal touch which would have put her completely at ease with her children, and in their early years she was too preoccupied with matters of sovereignty. Prince Albert also found that the call of duty and endless state papers frustrated his desire to spend as much time with his children as he liked. All the same, by and large it was a happy childhood for youngsters in the nursery at Buckingham Palace. Lady Lyttleton took care to ensure a steady balance between toys in the nursery – soldiers, dolls and tea sets – and more stimulating learning materials. Books of children's tales and songs were also provided and regularly used.

The general practice for children of middle- and upper-class parents in Victorian times was to be 'seen but not heard'. They generally lived in stuffy nursery quarters well away from the rest of the house, supervised dutifully by nursemaids, watched over by a governess, and given unappetizing meals with a high proportion of boiled vegetables and milk puddings. As a special treat, they might be allowed downstairs to the dining-room, when their parents had finished their meal, for a small piece of fruit or jelly. When older, they would be allowed to sit through a whole meal downstairs. Smaller children, however, might only see their parents for an hour or so in the day, when they were expected to behave like small, quiet adults.

The royal children of the 1840s were comparatively lucky. Regular references in the Queen's journal to her small sons and daughters quarrelling, fighting, and pulling each others' hair, are ample testimony to the fact that they had their full share of childish mischief which was checked as appropriate, if never entirely eliminated.

All of them were devoted to Lady Lyttelton, as a governess, with her forward-thinking attitude to punishment. As a small girl, Vicky – as the Princess Royal became, 'Pussy' evidently being thought too winsome and undignified for a growing child – started telling 'deliberate untruths' which was 'a very serious offence indeed'. She told her French governess Mlle Charrier that 'Laddle' had given her permission to wear her pink bonnet for an outing. When found out, she was 'imprisoned with tied hands and very seriously admonished and I trust was aware of her fault in the right way'.[29] Vicky did not seem unduly concerned when her solitary confinement ended, and her hands had not been tightly tied, but the punishment was enough to impress on her the error of her ways.

Every night Lady Lyttelton wrote a detailed report on the children, their diet, general health and mental progress. It was sent early next morning to the Queen, who read it at once. Much of it was taken up with details about the children's health. True to the fashion of the day, Dr Clark's recommendation was always the same, prompted by the local apothecary – 'a dose'. Lady Lyttelton ordered castor oil for the medicine cupboard every week, and packets of Gray's powder for soothing upset stomachs.

Diet was the subject of great attention. There was a fallacy that meat was dangerous and overheated the blood. If one of the children became too unruly, she cut out red meat for a day 'to cool them down'. Bertie and Alice were always hungry and rarely satisfied with first helpings, while Vicky's appetite was fitful. Easily distracted or upset, if unwell as a child she lost interest in food altogether. Dr Clark was blamed in the reports for interfering too much, and altering the diet so much that the children when small never got used to any taste in particular. Chicken broth, or mutton broth with a little meat, was given according to his whims, rather than the children's digestion.

Later they progressed to boiled beef and carrots, followed by plain rice or semolina pudding. Although this was typical Victorian child fare, some of the nursery maids were astonished at how simply the royal children ate. They declared that their families at home had far better, and they would never have believed their diet if they had not seen it at first hand for themselves. Or had they expected more for the great-nephews and great-nieces of that legendary glutton King George IV?

Queen Victoria and Prince Albert felt it was their duty to influence their children's religious beliefs. They had no patience with the fashionable theory which let children decide for themselves when they grew up. It was their responsibility, they considered, to present their opinions in a careful and straightforward way which would neither puzzle nor alarm young minds. According to the Queen's memorandum on the religious upbringing of her eldest daughter – to be followed by all of them in turn,

> It is quite certain she should have a great reverence for God and for religion but that she should have the feeling of devotion and love which our heavenly Father encourages His earthly children to have for Him, and not one of fear and trembling, and the thought of death and an after life should not be represented in a forbidding and alarming way, and that she should be made to know as yet no difference of creeds, and not think that she can only pray on her knees and that those who do not kneel are less fervent or devout in their prayers.[30]

She believed that it was the duty of a mother to give her children their first lesson in religion, which was 'best given to a child day by day at its mother's knee'. However, soon after Vicky's birth, she realized that other duties made this impossible. She regretted with some bitterness that she could not be with her daughter when she said her prayers at bedtime.

Queen Victoria's religious views were 'simple and straightforward'. In practice, she was a Low Church Anglican with a leaning towards Presbyterianism. Her favourite preacher was the Scottish Presbyterian divine Dr Macleod, whose sermons she kept by her and often quoted.

Prince Albert had been brought up as a Lutheran, though unlike most Lutherans with tolerance towards all faiths. He brought from Germany the custom of taking Holy Communion only three times a year, at Christmas, Easter and Whitsun. The English habit of kneeling in prayer seemed strange to him, but he taught his children that there was no significance in the posture they adopted, so long as they prayed with sincerity for strength to live according to the principles in which they believed. He allowed his children to kneel with Lady Lyttelton when they said their prayers with her.

Queen Victoria had always been brought up to take for granted the English custom of Sunday being a day not only of rest, but devoid of amusements altogether. Prince Albert changed all that in the family. On the first Sunday after his honeymoon, he had played chess with Stockmar, as usual, and he kept the habit up. Once, with a twinkle in his eye, he gave the Sabbatarian Archdeacon Wilberforce a crisis of conscience by inviting him to take part in a game of chess after he had preached the sermon at Windsor. However, all his efforts to enliven Sunday for the people at large were coldly received. Even though Queen Victoria supported her husband, public opinion would not allow brass bands to play in the London parks, or museums to be opened on Sundays. It savoured too much of foreign influence.

At least it was within his power to make sure his own family enjoyed Sundays. After Morning Service at Windsor, they would relax by playing games in the long corridor at the castle, or skating in winter, skittles on the lawn in summer, or taking the dogs for a walk.

In Novembr 1844 Wilberforce gave the Queen a booklet, *Scripture Reading Lessons for Little Children*, in which he had produced simplified adaptations of Bible readings to be read to the royal children. In his Preface, he remarked that the pages therein were 'intended to tell Children about Jesus Christ. To do this it was necessary to give a short account of man's creation in innocence, and of his fall into sin.'[31]

Lady Lyttelton was given a fairly free hand in bringing up the children. One great proviso was made; any sign of pride in the children must always be checked at once. The children must never think that because of their exalted birth they were better than others. Haughtiness was dealt with at once, and rudeness to servants was always punished. Good manners and consideration for all were paramount. If the children grumbled about having to wash their faces in cold water, they were reminded that the poor never washed in anything else. Complaints about having no bedroom of their own brought the retort that they were lucky not to live in slums where brothers and sisters shared the tiniest of rooms.

The Princesses were taught to take care of their clothes and keep them tidy. Kid gloves had to be blown into after being taken off, so they would not lose their shape. Bonnet ribbons were neatly rolled so they would be uncreased when next worn. Ribbons from the Queen's discarded hats were ironed out, and used to tie round the sleeves of her daughters' dresses. Domestic recycling had its place even in the nineteenth century.

The Queen and Prince Albert were full of ideas for the upbringing of their children, and never lacked advice from others. A few months after their marriage they composed a joint memorandum on the education and development of princes, full of lofty phrases about the 'moral and intellectual faculties of man', and strict instructions on hours of work, exercise and relaxation. Stockmar read it and declared gravely that any child subjected to such a regime would surely succumb to brain fever. Though German himself, he appreciated that much of the unpopularity of the education of King George III's sons had been as a result of their foreign education. These children, he insisted, must be educated in England.

On the other hand, Lord Melbourne maintained that King George IV and the Duke of York had been educated like English boys, by English schoolmasters, and according to the system of English schools. Whatever their faults, he declared, they were quite Englishmen; the others, who went abroad earlier and were schooled at European universities, were more foreign in their manner.

'Be not over solicitous about education,' he had advised the Queen (1 December 1841). 'It may be able to do much, but it does not do so much as is expected from it. It may mould and direct the character, but it rarely alters it.'[32]

His wise words were not heeded. Thanks to Stockmar's lofty memoranda, the Prince of Wales was to have an education which should 'in no wise tend to make him a demagogue, but a man of calm, profound, comprehensive understanding, with a deep conviction of the indispensable necessity of practical morality to the welfare of the Sovereign and People'.[33]

The unfortunate fact of the matter was that Bertie was a comparatively normal boy. Vicky, a precocious, gifted intellectual, took after her father. Her brother, as the Queen admitted, was her 'caricature'. Although he quickly outgrew a tendency to stutter, he evidently disliked his lessons, and thus compared unfavourably with his sister. Only the most brilliant of boys could have done otherwise.

Such frustration drove him to outbursts of childish anger. On occasion it needed two people to hold him down in case he did any harm to himself or one of the other children, either with his fists, a knife, or a pair of scissors from the nurse's workbox.[34] As he grew older, the 'fits' lasted longer and took more out of him. He would scream, stamp his feet, tear his books, and bite or scratch his sisters, kicking them and pulling their hair. When exhausted, he would lie down pale and panting for hours. Dr Clark assured the parents blandly that there was nothing to be alarmed about, but the less phlegmatic Stockmar warned Prince Albert that he should not leave Bertie alone with the younger children.

Lady Lyttelton was particularly fond of him. She appreciated that, beside his clever sister, he had been cast in the role of ugly duckling, and knew that he needed sympathy as well as understanding. When he was about a year old, she described him looking 'through his large clear blue eyes with a frequent very sweet smile'. At nearly two years of age, he was 'just as forward as the majority of children of his age, and no more'. But in August 1845, when he was three months away from his fourth birthday, she reported that he was 'uncommonly averse to learning and requires much patience from wilful inattention and constant interruptions, getting under the table, upsetting the books and sundry anti-studious practices'.[35] Thirteen months later, she noted with sadness that he had only reached the same standard of learning as four-year-old Princess Alice, who was 'neither studious nor so clever' as their elder sister.

The Princess Royal, whom she called 'Princessy', was 'all gracefulness and prettiness, very fat and active, running about and talking a great deal' but '*over* sensitive' and inclined to be temperamental. At eighteen months Prince Alfred showed signs of having 'a very good manly temper; much more like that of most children than that of the Princess Royal or Prince of Wales'. When he was four and a half, she wrote of his 'very uncommon abilities; and a mind which will make the task of instructing him most smooth and delightful'.[36]

Vicky was charmingly precocious. At the age of six, 'she begins to try one's depth, and talk blue,' Lady Lyttelton wrote (29 July 1847). 'Poor Roger Bacon! so hard upon him to have been thought wicked because he was so clever as to invent gunpowder!' Mention in lessons of the Caledonian Canal prompted the question – did Her Royal Highness understand the meaning of Caledonian? 'Oh yes; Caledonia meant formerly Scotland, so it is only a more *elegant* way of saying *Scotch*.'[37] A year later, when Bertie was showing Affie a picture book, he explained to the tutor Sarah Hildyard that his younger brother (then not quite four) did not know the story of Samson. Vicky broke in; 'Oh, you are quite right, dear Bertie – don't explain that to him. We must never do too much with young minds.'[38]

At first, the elder children shared the same teachers. Sarah Anne Hildyard, a clergyman's daughter, known to the children as 'Tilla', joined the nursery shortly before Vicky's fourth birthday. She saw that Vicky, like Bertie, was subject to rages and general insubordination out of sheer boredom. Lessons were therefore made a little more advanced. She devised a simulated schoolroom with a blackboard and maps.

A timetable was introduced for Vicky, starting at 8.20 a.m. with 'Arithmetic, Dictation, Poetry or Questions in History', and ending at 6 p.m. with 'Geography, history or Work Chronology as far as Edward 6th.' The final class was replaced twice a week by dancing lessons. Scripture was studied three times weekly, usually with the Queen, and reading, writing, French and German each day.[39] Miss Hildyard and Vicky read Gibbon's *Decline and Fall of the Roman Empire* together and, as each volume was published, Macaulay's *History of England*. The old precept of Princess Victoria of Kent's young days – that fiction was too frivolous – was disregarded. The 'improving' books of Mrs Sarah Trimmer, Maria Edgeworth and Hannah Moore, were banished, and popular novels of the day by Charles Dickens and others were introduced. Vicky had seen some of Shakespeare's plays with great enjoyment, full of praise for the acting of Macready, and she became a keen student of the printed texts. Miss Hildyard had always been interested in botany, and taught all the children how to recognize wild flowers.

Music was taught by Mrs Anderson, a gifted widow who had formerly been a concert pianist. Vicky made a fair pupil, though she disliked the drudgery of scales and five-finger exercises. Bertie had piano lessons, but never showed any musical talent.

Theatrical performances at Windsor Castle were an important part of the children's education, in addition to Prince Albert's efforts to establish some kind of court theatre in England parallel to that which he had known and enjoyed at Coburg. A small theatre was constructed in the castle, and all performances were given during the Christmas season. Initially the theatre was in the Rubens Room (later the King's Drawing-Room), but later moved to the adjacent, more spacious St George's Hall.

The children regularly joined guests and household in the audience, once they were considered old enough to find the plays of benefit. Occasionally they were quite carried away and almost forgot themselves. At a performance of *Henry IV, Part I* in November 1853, Bertie found Falstaff's soliloquy so hilarious that, 'as tears of laughter rolled down his cheeks in his ecstasy, he rolled up his tartan [kilt] and at the same time rubbed his knees with great gusto'. Sitting next to him, Vicky glanced in terror round the room, was relieved that nobody else appeared to have noticed, and swiftly gave the kilt a vigorous tug, 'which restored propriety and brought the happy boy to a sense of the situation'.[40]

3
'May it all turn to good!'

In April 1849 the next step of the Prince of Wales's education began. Henry Birch, aged thirty, a former captain of Eton who had gone on to become a master there for four years, after taking four university prizes at King's College, Cambridge, was engaged as the Prince's principal tutor, at a salary of £800 per annum.

The Prince had already been taught languages – English, French and German – by three mistresses who reported progress daily through Lady Lyttelton. Birch taught him English, geography, and calculating; assistant tutors were responsible for handwriting, drawing, religion, music, German, French, archaeology, science and history. Under this regime, it was said, the Prince enjoyed shorter holidays, and worked under greater pressure than any other schoolboy in the kingdom. Every weekday, including Saturday, was divided into five hourly or half-hourly periods. Lessons were never discontinued for more than a few days at a time. Family birthdays, however, were treated as holidays, and some relaxation occurred whenever the court moved from London or from Windsor.

Birch was warned about the Prince's rages, and took the news in his stride. He had, however, been used to dealing with normal boys at Eton. Almost at once, the Prince began to show the same signs of aversion to learning that he had in the nursery, becoming excitable and easily distracted. For a time, Birch was almost in despair of ever being able to teach him anything, and felt tempted to resign his post. But he became increasingly attached to his wayward pupil, who acquired considerable respect for him, and eventually found he was making progress.

Birch also had the heart to modify the severity of the regime. Riding and rowing on the lake were permitted, but for the most part 'recreation' consisted of afternoon walks, amateur theatricals and recitations. Birch was careful to restrict any teaching element during the walks, and had the forethought to introduce games calculated to appeal to the boy's imagination.

He stayed for nearly three years. In November 1849 he told the Queen and Prince Albert that he intended to take Holy Orders. The Queen assured him that it would not matter, as long as he promised not to be 'aggressive' – in other words, take to preaching fire and brimstone to his young pupil – and if he also promised to attend Presbyterian services while they were in Scotland, and to continue to participate in 'innocent amusements', like shooting, dancing and theatricals on Sundays. However, Prince Albert asked him to defer taking Holy Orders, in case he was tempted to attach greater importance to what he might consider that he owed to his cloth than to what the royal parents might consider best for the Prince of Wales's education.

By the time the Queen and Prince Albert celebrated their thirtieth birthdays in May and August 1849 respectively, they had six children. Three more were to follow. On 1 May 1850 Prince Arthur Patrick Albert was born. 'The children are all wild about "new brother," who has regular features and a fine complexion,' Lady Lyttelton wrote six days later. 'So here is another yet of the numberless instances of *perfect awful*, spotless prosperity which has been bestowed on this house. May it all turn to good!'[1]

This strong, healthy baby entered the world on the eighty-first birthday of the Duke of Wellington. Appropriately, the Duke stood as his godfather, and coincidentally it soon seemed likely that the boy would follow a military career. From the moment he could sit up and take notice he would clap his hands at the sight of a red coat, while the sound of a military band made him shriek with delight. Whenever they were at Windsor his nurse had to take him to the terrace every day to see the sentries marching backwards and forwards, and he could never bear to miss watching the changing of the guard at Buckingham Palace. On his first birthday he was thrilled to be given a toy drum, and his announcement that 'Arta is going to be a soldier' caused no surprise.

In November 1850 Lady Lyttelton retired. The four elder children had formed a close bond with her, and she was greatly moved by their childish farewells. The Prince of Wales, 'who has seen so little of me lately, cried and seemed to feel most'. She had been his most constant defender. The Princess Royal said 'many striking, feeling and clever things'. Princess Alice gave her a 'look of soft tenderness [which] I never shall forget; nor Prince Alfred with his manly face in tears, looking so pretty'.[2] Her successor was Lady Caroline Barrington, sister of Earl Grey.

In February 1852 Birch left his appointment as tutor to the Prince of Wales and took up Holy Orders. He felt he had 'found the Key to his heart'. He wrote of the Prince to Baron Stockmar (20 November 1850):

Taking into consideration the nature and disposition evinced by the Prince of Wales, will a change of tutor within a year be good or bad for him? . . . If his parents are dissatisfied with my treatment of him, as sometimes I have feared that they may be, and if they think that a fresh tutor would do the work better, well and good . . . If, on the contrary, they or you feel I can be of any service to the Prince of Wales by remaining with him beyond January 1852 I wish you would so far act out the part of a private friend as to tell me so.[3]

Stockmar and Prince Albert were less than pleased by this letter. It confirmed their intention to find another tutor at the end of the three years originally agreed, but as Birch was already committed to a new career, he had nothing to lose by plain speaking.

The Prince of Wales was greatly upset. Lady Canning, one of the Queen's ladies-in-waiting, noted: 'It has been a trouble and sorrow to the Prince of Wales, who has done no end of touching things since he heard that he was to lose him, three weeks ago. He is such an affectionate dear little fellow; his notes and presents which Mr Birch used to find on his pillow were really too moving.'[4]

In February 1852 Birch wrote a final report for Prince Albert. His pupil had been 'extremely disobedient, impertinent to his masters and unwilling to submit to discipline'. Extraordinarily selfish and unable to play at any game for five minutes, or attempt anything new or difficult, without losing his temper, he could not endure 'chaff', of any kind, 'but I thought it better, notwithstanding his sensitiveness, to laugh at him . . . and to treat him, as I know that boys would have treated him at an English public school, and as I was treated myself'. In time, he saw '*numerous* traits of a very amiable and affectionate disposition', but it was difficult to follow a systematic plan of management or regular course of study because he was 'so different on different days'. He continued to display symptoms of dumb insolence or mental collapse, during which he refused to answer questions to which he knew the answers perfectly well, but 'always evinced a most forgiving disposition after I had occasion to complain of him to his parents, or to punish him. He has a very keen perception of right and wrong, a very good memory, very singular powers of observation.'

Birch had been one of the first people to see that the Prince of Wales would learn from people, rather than from books. No intellectual, he would be a keen judge of character. The real problem, Birch underlined, was that he lacked contact with boys of his own age, and suffered from 'being continually in the society of older persons'. He had no standard by which to measure his own powers; 'nothing that a tutor can say, or even a parent, has such influence as intercourse with sensible boys of the same age, or a little older, unconsciously teaching by example. I always found that boys' characters at Eton were formed as much by contact with others as by the precepts of their tutors.'5 Moreover, the Prince was being completely deprived, not to say starved, of the encouragement and comradeship which a boy of his character desperately longed for.

The next tutor was Frederick Waymouth Gibbs, a Fellow of Trinity College and a barrister on the Northern Circuit. As Chancellor of Cambridge University, Prince Albert had consulted Sir James Stephen, Professor of Modern History at Cambridge (and grandfather of the novelist Virginia Woolf), about possible tutors for his two eldest sons. Gibbs had been brought up with Sir James's sons, his own mother being hopelessly insane and his father financially ruined. He was engaged to become tutor to the two elder Princes, at an annual salary of £1,000, 'with any addition to that sum which Baron Stockmar may decide to be just and reasonable.'

On their first walk, the Prince of Wales apologized to Gibbs for the low spirits of himself and Prince Alfred. 'The Prince of Wales thought it necessary to make a sort of apology in his walk for his sorrow: "You cannot wonder if we are somewhat dull to-day. We are sorry Mr Birch is gone. It is very natural, is it not?" The Prince is conscious of owing a great deal to Mr Birch and really loves and respects him,'6 Gibbs noted woodenly in his diary.

One of the first tasks which fell to Gibbs was to tell the Prince of Wales his destiny. As the son of a Queen regnant, and younger than his formidably clever and much-admired sister, it was perhaps natural that he should assume Vicky would be their mother's heir. The tutor evidently did not explain the succession very clearly to the puzzled young boy, who was so confused that he went and asked the Queen. 'He generally lets out to me, when he walks with me, something or other, that is occupying his mind,' she noted in her journal (12 February 1852). He told her that he had always believed Vicky would succeed her. 'I explained to him the different successions . . . He took it all in, very naturally.'[7]

Unlike Birch, Gibbs placed less value on the affection of his charges than on making a good impression on his employers. Under instructions from Prince Albert, he extended the Prince of Wales's lessons to cover six or seven hourly periods between 8 a.m. and 6 p.m., six days a week. These periods were divided so as not to exceed more than two hours' continuous application at a time. The Princes learnt Latin, acted in French and German plays, and were instructed to read selected classics from English, French and German literature. Arithmetic, algebra and geometry were taught, with direct reference to 'their applications to Gunnery, Fortifications and the Mechanical Arts'.

In addition, the Prince of Wales was also made to study chemistry 'and its kindred sciences, with the Arts dependent upon them'. He also composed essays on ancient and modern historical problems, in English, French and German. He prepared maps to illustrate his reading, and studied the principles of 'Social Economy'. Finally, he was required to study music and drawing as both arts were vital to the education of a prince. As if that was not enough, Gibbs was ordered to ensure that the boys were physically exhausted at the end of every day through riding, drill, and gymnastics.

Within a few days it was obvious that the system was asking too much of the Prince. Entries in Gibbs's diary to his young charge throwing stones in his face, running about during lessons, making faces and spitting, and 'a great deal of bad words', became commonplace. Queen Victoria was puzzled to notice symptoms of acute exhaustion in her son, and called Gibbs's attention to his hanging his head and looking at his feet, and 'fits of nervous and unmanageable temper'. She thought that he had been 'injured by being with the Princess Royal, who was very clever and a child far above her age. She puts him down by a word or a look, and their mutual affection had been, she feared, impaired by this state of things.'[8]

The three men who worked under Gibbs all protested that the Prince was being driven too hard. Gerald Wellesley, the domestic chaplain responsible for the Princes' religious education, and later Dean of Windsor, warned Gibbs that Prince Albert's system had overtaxed the boy's strength; their object should be 'to instruct him without overworking him'. Dr Voisin, the French master, warned that the Prince would be worn out too early. 'Make him climb trees! Run! Leap! Row! Ride!' In many aspects, he thought, 'savages are much better educated than we are'. If left to himself, the Prince would be 'a splendid boy'. Dr Becker, Prince Albert's librarian, bravely warned the Prince that his son's regular fits of blind destructive rage were a natural reaction to a system of education which placed too great and continuous a strain on a young mind and body. More breaks in his study, more encouragement and less in the way of high expectations, and no irony or mockery when his parents had to correct the Prince of Wales, were the answer.

Nevertheless Gibbs was convinced that he, Stockmar and Prince Albert were correct. The Queen thought that he was in every way more satisfactory and 'agreeable' than the well-meaning Mr Birch had ever been.

Only on one matter did the obsequious Gibbs beg to differ from his royal employers. The Prince of Wales's isolation, he warned, was harmful. While Queen Victoria and Prince Albert had always sought to remind their children that they were no better than their subjects, merely luckier by an accident of birth, they hesitated to admit companions to Buckingham Palace and Windsor Castle, because they had convinced themselves that companionship would lead to friendship, and thus into 'an impermissible relationship of equality'. Gibbs persisted, adamant that the experiment would be of great educational value. In due course, from summer 1852 onwards, a few carefully selected companions were permitted to come from Eton to Windsor Castle to play or ride with the royal children.

One, Charles Wynne-Carrington, later looked back with some

acerbity on the 'experiment'. While Gibbs was careful to put on a display of kindness to the Princes, it was evident that both boys were very strictly treated and brought up. He could see that Prince Alfred was 'the favourite', but he always liked the Prince of Wales better, as he 'had such an open generous disposition and the kindest heart imaginable. He was a very plucky boy and always ready for fun which often got him into scrapes. He was afraid of his father who seemed a proud, shy, stand-offish man, not calculated to make friends easily with children. I was frightened to death of him.'[9]

Affie admired his elder brother, and was a good influence on him by drawing him into family games. Bertie only lost his temper and bullied the others when he was bored and frustrated. Unhappily, Bertie's influence tended to lead Affie to copy him, so that on bad days Gibbs found himself with two rude, inattentive pupils instead of one. When Affie found himself being kicked, having his hair pulled, and even occasionally threatened with a paper knife, self-defence was the only answer. As he was bigger than his elder brother, if not physically tougher as well, he could look after himself.

From October 1851 to May 1855 Affie kept a journal, dictated to Birch and then to Gibbs. Like his mother's childhood journal, it lacks spontaneity, but is not without its useful insights into royal childhood. One of the earliest entries, from November 1851, records his delight at being given 'a most beautiful watch', a present from the Duchess of Kent, from the Great Exhibition; 'Mr Birch told me I make good use of my time, and that I had a watch which would show me how quickly minutes and hours fly away.'[10]

At Christmas that year, spent at Windsor, he recorded various presents – 'a sword, a Tyrolese hat and belt, some very pretty soldiers which I shared with Bertie' – and a visit with Bertie and Mr Birch to the castle kitchens on Christmas Day, 'and I saw the Baron of beef and boar's head, and I went down to the larder where I saw hares, pheasants, grouse and a great quantity of fat meat; and we saw the pastry room and a model of Windsor Castle in sugar. In the evening Bertie and I supped with our sisters in the Oak Room and played with some of the presents. When I had finished playing I went to the great dinner and had a very happy evening.'[11]

In the following year he noted visits to the British Museum, Westminster Abbey, and an exhibition of lion hunter George Gordon-Cumming's exploits from his travels in South Africa, a display which gave lifelong inspiration to the boy who would become the most widely travelled member of the family and set foot in all five continents by the age of twenty-five.

Who had the final word over more stringent aspects of the children's upbringing? Prince Albert and Stockmar were not entirely to blame. As far as possible, the Prince tried to treat his children as equals. Although they were all a little in awe of him, except for the Princess Royal, they all appreciated how fond he was of them, and could penetrate the man behind the reserve. They knew that he loved them, appreciated and needed their company, more than the Queen herself.

As she admitted in a letter to Princess Augusta of Prussia (6 October 1856), a year after the Princess Royal had become engaged to Augusta's son, Prince Frederick William, she found 'no especial pleasure or compensation in the company of the elder children'. Only very rarely did she 'find the rather intimate intercourse with them either agreeable or easy. . . . Firstly, I only feel properly *à mon aise* and quite happy when Albert is with me; secondly, I am used to carrying on my many affairs quite alone; and then I have grown up all alone, accustomed to the society of adult (and never with younger) people – lastly, I still cannot get used to the fact that Vicky is almost grown up. To me she still seems the same child, who had to be kept in order and therefore must not become too intimate.'[12]

In conversation with Lord Clarendon in December 1858, the Prince expressed reservations over what he called the Queen's 'aggressive' system: 'he had always been embarrassed by the alarm which he felt lest the Q's mind should be excited by any opposition to her will; and that, in regard to the children, the disagreeable office of punishment had always fallen on him'.[13] The shadow of King George III, and the fear that too much 'excitement' if provoked could deprive his granddaughter of her reason, was sufficient to keep Prince Albert in check.

Did he disagree with Gibbs's plan to allow their sons to fraternize with boys from Eton? He might not have approved, but the main opposition to Gibbs's scheme certainly came from the Queen. She had 'a great fear of young and carefully brought up Boys mixing with older Boys and indeed with any Boys in general, for the mischief done by bad boys and the things they may hear and learn from them cannot be overrated.'[14]

Queen Victoria's youngest son was born on 7 April 1853. The birth was made easier by chloroform, administered by the anaesthetist Dr John Snow of Edinburgh, under the supervision of Sir James Clark, and the Queen recovered rapidly. She decided to call him Leopold, after his great-uncle, King of the Belgians, whom she informed that following childbirth she had never been so well, and that the child was 'a jolly fat little fellow, but no beauty'.

Unfortunately he did not thrive like the others. The 'jolly fat little fellow' quickly became thin, with a feeble cry and a frequent tendency to be sick. The Queen decided he should have a wet-nurse from the Highlands. When Mrs Macintosh arrived, not speaking a word of English, she was sure he would improve. Wet-nurses could be a problem; the one engaged for the Prince of Wales, Mary Ann Brough, had become morose and 'stupid', and a year after Prince Leopold's birth, the Queen was horrified to hear that she had murdered her own six children.

Dr Clark attributed Leopold's failure to thrive to a weak digestion, and suggested a change of wet-nurse, whose milk was less rich. A shipwright's wife was found, appropriately, in Cowes. For a few weeks he improved. However when he began to walk, and fell down frequently, it was seen that he bruised much more easily than the others, and cried out in pain. 'Little Leo', it was discovered, suffered from haemophilia, the bleeding disease transferred from a female to a male, in which bleeding cannot be stopped.

The source of haemophilia in the royal family was thought to have been a spontaneous mutation in the genes inherited by Queen Victoria from her mother. No instances of it were traced in the Duchess of Kent's relations. Prince Leopold was the only victim in her family and the only male transmitter. Two of her daughters, Alice and (the as yet unborn) Beatrice, were carriers, and through them it spread to several of the royal houses of Europe, with disastrous consequences for the royal and imperial families of Spain and Russia into which the princesses married.

Queen Victoria tried to protect her 'child of anxiety' from accidents by too much care. Not surprisingly, he reacted against this by resisting, behaving recklessly, and wanting to behave as normally as his brothers and sisters.

He made up for being delicate by an unquenchable spirit and an intellect which gave signs of being as marked as that of his eldest sister. He learned to read with ease, and was rarely to be seen with his nose out of a book. Like his eldest sister, he enjoyed confounding his elders with questions of an intellectual nature to which he knew the answers. At the age of five he wanted to know all about the paintings on the walls of his father's study at Osborne, and showed a precocious knowledge of Italian art.

Prince Albert knew better than anyone else how to treat Leopold. Although just as perplexed and worried as the Queen about his haemophilia, he apparently assumed – or pretended to assume – that the boy would grow out of it, as he would out of the epilepsy which attacked him before he was a year old. He carried 'little Leo' in his arms, so he could see what the others were doing, but it was frustrating for both that he could not join in their games. Some days the boy had to lie on a sofa to recover from what would have been a minor accident in the others but a potential crisis in his case. To occupy his mind, Prince Albert would let him use his paintbox, and help to guide his hand as he discovered for himself the joy of creating his own watercolours.

He had a pronounced musical ear, and responded keenly to Mrs Anderson's piano lessons. It soon became apparent that he had a passion for music, and had a strong singing voice. Father and son would in time sing duets with great enjoyment. When Leopold was confined to bed, Albert was careful not to show that he felt sorry for him, and as far as possible he always behaved as if there was nothing unusual in his being kept apart from the other children. It was the only way, he realized, to help the boy try and lead as normal a life as his condition would allow.

Queen Victoria and Prince Albert both disliked London. The crowds, polluted air, and for the Queen the city's constant associations with the unhappiness of her childhood, and for Albert the sweeter memories of rural tranquillity in the Coburg he had left behind, led them to seek retreats further afield.

Though Windsor Castle was something of a retreat from London, they found nothing homely about the vast building. They had continued to use the Royal Pavilion at Brighton, King George IV's exotic creation which had also been stayed in, less willingly, by King William IV. Neither of them liked it, and the last straw came one day in 1845 when a crowd of two hundred pursued them as they walked from the pavilion to the chain pier. Some people even ran alongside the Queen and peered under her bonnet. They never returned to the pavilion, which was sold to the Brighton Corporation in 1850.

At the suggestion of Sir Robert Peel, who had heard of an estate on the Isle of Wight for sale, in 1845 they purchased a new 'Marine Residence', Osborne House, with an estate of 1,000 acres. The existing house was too small, and it was demolished to make way for a new mansion, designed by Prince Albert and the London builder Thomas Cubitt. The foundation stone of the Pavilion Wing, the first part they would occupy, was laid in June 1845. Fifteen months later they took up residence there, and within five years, the two eastern wings (accommodation for the household) were completed.

Osborne was designed very much with the children in mind. More than anywhere else, its arrangement and facilities still retain the flavour, the essence of childhood at the Victorian court. Queen Victoria and Prince Albert had their private apartments on the first floor. Below were the official audience and reception rooms, in which a homely atmosphere was added by Mary Thornycroft's statues of the children dressed as characters from Thomson's *The Seasons*; above, on the second floor, were the nursery quarters.

The children generally remained in the nursery until they were six, when they graduated to the schoolroom on the first floor. Two rooms in the nursery suite were the governess's sitting-room and bedroom respectively, divided by folding doors. The children each had their own individual high-backed chair, topped with a shield inlaid with its royal owner's initials, while there were also smaller chairs with Berlin wool-work seats embroidered by the Queen's aunt Mary, Duchess of Gloucester, last surviving child of King George III. Next door was the nursery bedroom, containing cots with hinged canework sides and upholstered pads to protect the children. They were perhaps designed partly by their father. There was plenty of room for toys as well, most of which – rocking horses, dolls' houses and clockwork mechanical devices from Germany – it can be assumed were loved, and worn to bits, by grandchildren and great-grandchildren. A wicker trug owned by Louise, who was destined never to have children of her own to pass it down to, still survives on display in the nursery.

Osborne was relatively close to London, but secluded, and close to the sea with a private beach for bathing and boating. It was thus ideal for bringing up a young family. With its wooded views, spacious grounds and views across the Solent, it was an excellent holiday home for them all. The children learned to swim in the bay, using either the small pier or, later, the swimming bath, made from pontoons, with a wooden grating floor open to the sea. Each fine summer day would find parents and children aboard the royal yacht *Victoria and Albert*, or the smaller steam yacht *Fairy*. There was always something to keep everyone on board occupied, whether looking out to sea through their father's telescope, sketching on deck, or pretending to steer.

Affie, who adored anything to do with the sea, was particularly in his element at Osborne. An excellent swimmer, he revelled in the outdoor life and, being naturally darker in colouring than the rest, tanned easily. With his mechanical mind, he quickly mastered the essentials of the *Fairy*, and was more effective than his father at fixing any minor faults. So did Helena, the tomboy of the girls, who also had a knack with machinery. She and Affie both studied the motors and machinery with interest, never minding how dirty or greasy their hands became in the process.

Princess Helena, or 'Lenchen', as she was always to be known *en famille*, was a placid, even-tempered child. She had none of the obstinacy or tendency to answer back of her eldest sister Victoria, the precocious, self-willed Princess Royal, and none of Alice's tendency to be easily crushed. Bertie and Affie were quick to realize that any attempts at teasing or bullying her would result in a short sharp blow where it hurt. Lady Augusta Bruce, lady-in-waiting, noted that at six years of age the Princess 'resented much being called a Baby by her eldest brother and threatened to slap his face if he persisted!'[15]

To the children, a never-ending delight of Osborne was the Swiss Cottage. Prince Albert had always loved the *Schweizerei*, or

Swiss Dairy Farm, at his childhood home, Rosenau. Though it was long assumed that the cottage was a prefabricated building manufactured abroad and imported in sections prior to being erected at Osborne, it was more probable that the estate carpenters constructed the buildings themselves, possibly with assistance from a Continental carpenter, or under the Prince's guidance.* It was made to imperial measurements, with basic overall dimensions of twenty-five feet by fifty feet, and erected on a rubble plinth about half a mile east of the house. The external logs, nine inches square, were initially coated with burnt umber, and later blackened with tar.

The children laid the foundation stone in 1853, and the completed dwelling was presented to them on 24 May 1854, their mother's thirty-fifth birthday. The first floor balcony and other details were in imitation of a traditional Swiss-style farmhouse. The interior was scaled down to child-size in every detail, with a fully-equipped kitchen and range. Here the Princes could learn carpentry and gardening, the Princesses housekeeping and cookery. Family parties were held in the dining-room on the first floor with an informality which was out of the question at the house. Miniature tea, dinner and dessert services, with plates inscribed 'SPARE NOT, WASTE NOT, WANT NOT', were used by the royal children for many years.

Much of the furniture and ornaments were collected by Prince Albert, mainly from Lucerne. They included a *secretaire*, or writing desk, embellished with wood carvings of rural Swiss life. Less homely was a carved table incorporating an ornate engraving, captioned '*DIE SOHNAE EDUARDUS IV*', in which the young Princes in the Tower were about to be smothered as they lay sleeping. Perhaps the lesson was not lost on Queen Victoria's young sons that they were lucky not to have lived in medieval times.

In one room there was a doll's house grocery shop, 'Spratt, Grocer to Her Majesty', where they learned the prices of everyday

---

* Restoration work carried out in 1990 showed that the wood used was *Pinus strobus*, a long-leafed pine found in North America. One of the European pines would have been more usual in a native Swiss or German building.

goods. The commodities on display included coffee, cocoa, several different kinds of tea, a selection of British wines, 'currie' powder and other spices, dried and crystallized fruits, and isinglass, or gelatine originally made from the air-bladders of freshwater fish. In the sitting-room upstairs a space was set aside for a small natural history museum containing fossils, and geological and botanical specimens, collected by the children on their father's instructions.

Garden plots near the cottage were laid out for each child, with spades, forks, wheelbarrows and trolleys marked with their initials, to forestall arguments: P.o.W., Pss.R., Pss.A., P.A., Pss.H., Pss.L. and so on. Their work was professionally criticized, and they were paid by the hour. They were taught how to erect tents, and make bricks.

Behind the cottage a miniature earth fort with redoubts (detached earthworks) was completed in 1856, on the suggestion of Prince Albert who had enjoyed playing in mock forts at Coburg with his brother. The Princes helped to construct the fort as a birthday surprise for Queen Victoria under the supervision of Affie's governor, Lieutenant John Cowell. In 1860 Arthur assisted in adding the brick-built Albert Barracks inside the fort, and a drawbridge was added the following year. It remained a source of fascination for him and succeeding generations of royal children throughout the rest of the century.

In the meantime, a first visit to Scotland in 1842 had marked the beginning of the Queen's love affair with her northern kingdom. She and her husband were immediately enchanted with the Scottish landscape (which reminded Albert of his native Thuringia, although his brother Prince Ernest pooh-poohed the comparison as a symptom of romantic fantasy), and respected the Highlanders for their simple manners and lack of pretence. The idea of having their own retreat in Scotland, far less accessible than the Isle of Wight, appealed to them. In 1848 they purchased a lease of the small castle of Balmoral, Deeside, and bought the property outright in 1852.

All the children revelled in Balmoral. To start with, it meant travelling to the Highlands by night on a train, at what then seemed the daredevil speed of 30 m.p.h., with a break in the journey to see the historic sights of Edinburgh. Once they arrived at their Deeside home, the fresh, sharp air gave them plenty of energy and kept them in good spirits. They enjoyed long pony expeditions across the hills which lasted up to a whole day, accompanied by a luncheon basket. The Queen and her daughters took their sketch-books, and once the eleven-year-old Princess Royal had to be rescued by one of the Scottish keepers after she sat on a wasps' nest. Prince Albert and his sons went deer-stalking and shooting, or on botanical explorations. In the evening there was dancing to the sound of bagpipes.

On a visit to Edinburgh in 1822 King George IV had gratified local sensibilities by wearing Highland costume, and his niece and her family likewise adopted the appropriate dress. In doing so, they helped to set a trend. All the children wore kilts, which were handed down to the younger ones irrespective of sex. Till the age of five, the Princes as well as their sisters had worn frocks, the only difference being that the boys' were pleated, while the girls' were gored. Helena generally took the part of a boy in theatricals; paintings of the children by Winterhalter usually showed her in Highland dress, with her hair parted at the side like her brothers. Highland costume became the generally accepted formal dress for the Princes when they appeared on public events; the Prince of Wales was thus attired when he and the Princess Royal accompanied their parents to the opening of the Great Exhibition at Crystal Palace in May 1851.

As a result, kilts for boys became fashionable among the middle classes. People only had to see a colour print of the Prince of Wales in Highland dress at the opening of the Great Exhibition, or some similar public function, to be inspired to follow the trend. Kilts could be handed down to younger sons, and they did not wear out or go out of fashion. Moreover, the concept of bare knees above the socks satisfied traditional Victorian notions of manliness and 'hardening' the wearer. They were less popular in the south of England, where they were generally reserved for formal occasions, if worn at all. Some families disliked the velvet jacket with its expensive silver buttons, while in some cases the would-be English wearer found it too much like fancy dress.

A by-product of Queen Victoria's love of everything Scottish was the popularity of tartan in mid-nineteenth-century Britain. The middle classes were equally entranced by its association with the 'romantic Highlands'. Its large checks showed to advantage on wide skirts and dresses for child and adult alike, silk tartans being made up into dresses for the Princesses.

Alice particularly enjoyed the freedom of Balmoral, especially visiting the cottagers without ceremony. Among the children, she was the most sensitive to the sufferings of others. Though outwardly exuberant, particularly in the family theatricals, her exterior hid a more introspective personality, with a particular desire to help others, whether it was visiting the wounded in hospitals at home during the Crimean War, or visiting the cottagers to distribute food and clothing. She also enjoyed riding her pony over the hills. So did Princess Helena, who went out in all weathers, never minding the rain, coming back soaking wet but all the better – and more hungry – for the experience.

That all the children, apart from the haemophiliac Leopold, enjoyed good health was no accident. Prince Albert was never particularly strong, and a martyr to perpetual stomach upsets, sore throats and swollen glands. The Queen had inherited her Hanoverian forebears' good health, but improved living standards played a part in their children's health. They all had healthy hair, good teeth, excellent complexions, and none suffered from bandy legs or rickets. Under Prince Albert's thorough regime, the kitchens and drainage systems at Windsor and Buckingham Palace were reorganized. Typhoid fever and diphtheria, infectious diseases which often started as a result of unhealthy conditions, claimed the lives of many young children in Victorian England – but not in the royal household. Ironically it was typhoid which caused his own death, while seventeen years later (to the very day) one of his daughters in Germany succumbed to diphtheria.

Osborne and Balmoral were built on modern lines with good sewerage, plenty of lavatories and bathrooms, and the luxury of running hot and cold water for family and servants alike; baths were plumbed in to drain as well. Much time was spent in these holiday homes, and the children caught few of the normal infectious childhood diseases. Bertie often suffered from a running nose in babyhood, and there were outbreaks of measles in 1853 and a mild form of scarlet fever in 1855, but otherwise they escaped serious epidemics. The parents attributed much to the sea air and bathing at Osborne and immunity of the 'hardening effect of the salt on the constitution'. Hot summer days at Osborne, where the family generally spent between sixty and ninety days each year, encouraged a routine which included breakfasting outside as frequently as possible.

Queen Victoria was always impervious to cold. She agreed with Stockmar, whose experience of practising medicine had instilled in him the conviction that warm temperatures encouraged germs and sickness. Cold baths and open windows were taken all the year round. The Queen liked to say that all her children took after her, though they did not. Vicky suffered from chilblains, particularly after her marriage when she lived in Germany, while Alice and Beatrice became very rheumatic. Few of the servants shared this dislike of heat. Lady Lyttelton, for one, had always relished being able to retire from the well-ventilated if not chilly nursery to her own room and roaring fire.

Another regular excitement for the children was the prospect of a cruise on board the *Victoria and Albert*. Sometimes they sailed around the coast of southern England. In August 1846 the two elder children were taken for an 'aquatic excursion' along the coast of south Devon, and to Guernsey. Vicky had inherited her mother's ability to sail well, and despite occasional bouts of seasickness at first, amused everybody by rushing around in high spirits until asked how she was feeling. Then she would lie down and pull a grimace in imitation of her mother's ladies, moaning, 'I'm very ill'.

In July 1852 Affie was on board another cruise along the south coast, and his journal was full of nautical observation, as befitted a future Admiral of the Fleet. They cruised past Plymouth up the Tamar on board the *Fairy*:

We passed the Dock Yard: there were a great many ships in front of the Dock Yards: they had not got any rigging, and were rather white looking on account of not being painted for service. We saw a lead mine from the 'Fairy' which we were told was 700 ft. deep; we have got some ore from it. The river was very dirty and full of mud, so that the 'Fairy' had to dig through till at last we could not go any further. When we came down we went close under the shore of the Harbour and the batteries saluted.[16]

Theatricals and *tableaux vivants* were regularly staged by the children, partly for the amusement of their parents, household and a few invited guests, and partly as an extension of their French and German classes. The French governess Madame Rolande was often *metteur-en-scène*, and Prince Albert generally supervised their efforts overall. Records show that no English plays were performed by the children in his lifetime, and performances were usually on Twelfth Night, or as close to his and the Queen's wedding anniversary (10 February) as possible.

The favourite choice at first was usually Racine's *Athalie*, which had just gained a new lease of life as a result of incidental music composed by Mendelssohn, a great favourite of the royal family. First staged at Windsor on the Queen's twelfth wedding anniversary in 1852, the play was quite a demanding one for a juvenile cast. Queen Athalie was portrayed by the Princess Royal, while Alice played both the grand priest Joad and his wife Josabeth, and the Prince of Wales was given the minor role of Abner. The set was the same as that used for a performance of *Julius Caesar* by Charles Kean and William Macready two years earlier, and the young royal players wore specially designed costumes 'of fine merino, with gold and silver braid'. The text was heavily cut 'and curtailed to avoid tediousness and to enable the Children to act it', and naturally the performance won the Queen's unqualified approval. She recorded in her journal that evening that 'Vicky looked very well and spoke and acted her long and difficult part . . . really admirably, with immense expression and dignity and with the true French emphasis, which indeed they all did', while 'Alice was 'méconnaissable' as the Priest, with a white beard and hair. She acted beautifully, Affie very nicely and Bertie very well, but his Roman armour was a little too big for him.'[17]

The same play was performed again three times between 10 and 13 January 1853 in the Tapestry Room at Windsor. A fuller version of the text was used, and the cast was augmented by members of two court families, the Phipps and the Seymours. The dress rehearsal and 'first night' were very successful, with Vicky giving a splendid performance at the climax of the play, 'the scene of fury, where she rushes out in a rage, extremely well'. However, she let matters down on the last performance, when she forgot much of her part.

Athalie was accordingly dropped from the repertoire. A number of more lighthearted German plays were introduced. Among them was *Das Hahnenschlag* (*The Cockshy*), which included two songs by the children, and a piece from Beethoven's Pastoral Symphony, played by Dr Barker behind the scenes. Another was *Die Tafelbirnen* (*The Pears*), by Agnes Frantz, 'a charming childish little piece'. Also judged a success was *Les Deux Petits Savoyards*, performed on 16 January 1854, in which the title roles were taken by Alice and Affie, while Vicky had the most important part, 'Madame la Marquise de Verseuil' in whose castle the action took place, and Bertie 'Le Bailli'. 'It was most successful and was very pretty and our Children did their parts extremely well,' the Queen wrote in her journal. 'Bertie (whom his father had painted to look quite hideous) acted with great spirit, and dear little Lenchen was incomparable as Clement, so important, never making a mistake. Everyone was inclined to laugh when she appeared, but she did not perceive it.'[18]

Almost as spectacular as these performances was a *tableau vivant* performed in February 1854 on their parents' fourteenth wedding anniversary, based on James Thomson's nineteenth-century blank verse epic *The Seasons*. Alice was Spring, scattering flowers as she delivered her speech. The Princess Royal was Summer with Arthur asleep among the cornsheaves, Alfred was Autumn, dressed as Bacchus in a leopard skin and crowned with grapes, and the Prince of Wales represented Winter, as an old man with a long white beard, his cloak covered with snow and icicles hanging from his hat, while Louise accompanied him in a Russian costume, sitting before a fire. At the closing scene, they gathered in a group with Helena appearing in clouds in a white robe, holding a cross. She delivered a speech in verse composed for the occasion, in which she proclaimed herself as Christ-loving Helena who had come to bless 'this auspicious day and tender their homage to their parents'.

After it was over, Prince Albert called to them to come out and jump down from the stage. The curtain was drawn up, but one of them remarked sadly, 'We can't get through the atmosphere', the gauze behind which they were acting. The gauze was pushed aside, and the Queen was so shocked at Arthur's scanty clothing that she sent him away to be dressed, despite an assurance by the nurse that he was wearing 'flesh-coloured decencies'. He was brought back a few moments later, the only apparent difference being a pair of socks that hardly came above his ankles.[19]

In this aspect, at least, Queen Victoria and Prince Albert were indeed typical Victorians. They might have been at pains to ensure that their children were well versed in language and literature, but where sex was concerned they took the customary nineteenth-century view. There was time enough for the children to find out when they were married – but not before.

Though the Queen found the stares of her elder children at her expanding figure disconcerting during her last two pregnancies, neither she nor Prince Albert were in a hurry to take the bull by the horns and explain to them exactly why. His insistence that their two elder sons should be physically and mentally exhausted after a day with their tutors, and his close supervision of the mixing with boys at Eton, were probably a consequence of his vain intention to keep impure thoughts at bay. That he himself was the one paragon of sexual virtue in a family of rakes, and that Queen Victoria's uncles and aunts had hardly set an example of saintly living to the nation, apparently eluded him.

The human body was a fit subject to be idealized in art, and art alone. For his thirty-first birthday, Queen Victoria presented her husband with a large painting by Winterhalter, *Florinda*, based on a scene from medieval Spanish literature in which a girl and her maidens in a palace garden, removing their clothes to bathe, were watched by Rodrigo, King of the Spanish Visigoths. With its generous portrayal of voluptuous nudes, Queen Victoria recorded in her journal (3 April 1852) that it was 'a most lovely picture containing a group of beautiful women'.[20] Naked flesh in the canvases of Winterhalter and William Dyce (whose large fresco of *Neptune resigning the Empire of the Seas to Britannia*, commissioned by Prince Albert, displayed several naked allegorical figures on the walls at Osborne), and statues in the classical tradition, were permitted, but that was all. The Princes and Princesses were not allowed to stay in the same room as each other without an adult being present, presumably in case they discovered anything unseemly. Once they had outgrown infancy, none of them ever saw their mother in bed until her last few months, when she was too elderly and infirm to care.

Some of her daughters, if not her sons, apparently inherited this prudery. As a young adult Vicky, three times a mother, could write modestly to her own mother (30 October 1862) that at Palermo she and her husband had seen children and young men who 'seem to dispense with clothing as much as possible. I saw some approaching a state of nature which made one rather shy to look at.'[21] Nevertheless, she and Alice were less squeamish than their mother, particularly when the ravages of war in Germany during the 1860s called on them to help nurse the wounded. Alice's keen interest in human anatomy, albeit for medical reasons, revolted the Queen, who declared firmly that such matters were far too indelicate for the female mind and eye.

Most of the children had been too young to appreciate the significance of the year of revolutions. The first public event which really made an impact on them was the death of the Duke of Wellington in September 1852. Though he was aged eighty-three, his demise was scarcely unexpected, but the Queen, her family and the nation were likewise plunged into deepest mourning for their national hero. Two-year-old Arthur wandered around sadly for weeks, talking about 'The Duke of Wellikon, little Arta's godpapa', while according to the Duchess of Kent's lady-in-waiting, Lady Augusta Bruce, 'The Queen has felt it *deeply*, and all the dear children enter into it with the heart and comprehension they have, the darlings.'[22]

Eighteen months later, Britain and France were at war with Russia. The Crimean War lasted two years, and for the children it was their first experience of what war meant to a belligerent nation. Vicky and Alice accompanied the Queen on hospital visits, and were moved by the physical suffering and mutilation they witnessed. When Lord Raglan paid a brief visit to Buckingham Palace, Vicky seized his arm, entreating him to 'hurry back to Sebastopol and take it or else you will kill Mama'. Lord Cardigan was invited by the Queen to Windsor Castle on his return from the Crimea after the charge of the Light Brigade. All the children (except Leopold, not yet aged two) were enthralled when he showed them a watercolour of the event, and related his experiences at first hand.*

*A group portrait of Lord Cardigan, the Queen, Prince Albert and their children at Windsor, was painted by James Sant. So persistent were the growing scandals and controversy surrounding Cardigan that the Queen commanded that her portrait should be painted out.[23]

The Patriotic Fund for the dependants of soldiers fighting in the Crimea, set up soon after the outbreak of war, also provided the children with a practical means of helping the war effort. In April 1855 an exhibition of paintings by amateur artists was staged at the Bond Street premises of the picture dealer Ernest Gambart. An instant success, it was transferred to Burlington House, Piccadilly, the following month, where it remained until July.

The Queen had given permission for her children to contribute work, and pride of place went to the Princess Royal's striking watercolour, *The Field of Battle*. She had originally intended to show a wounded Greek warrior attended by a maiden, but on the suggestion of Edward Corbould, official instructor in drawing and watercolour painting to the royal children, she substituted a British grenadier for the warrior. The *Illustrated London News* art critic described it as 'by far the best drawing in the room. . . . The composition is artistic, the sentiment poetic, and the execution spirited.'[24] It sold for 250 guineas at an auction in aid of the fund, and prints in chromolithography were sold for one guinea each. The Prince of Wales contributed a drawing of a knight in armour, which realized 55 guineas, while pictures by Alfred of *The Prince of Wales, afterwards Henry V*, Alice of *Prayer*, and Helena of *Girl asleep*, went for 30 guineas each.

Much of the credit for their drawing went to Edward Henry Corbould, who had been appointed their instructor in drawing and painting in watercolours in 1852. His skill in drawing, and inspiration for the children to copy his work before they were ready to produce their own original compositions, was not to be underestimated.

In April 1855 Napoleon III and Eugenie, Emperor and Empress of the French, paid a state visit to England. The children were unaccustomed to such 'bustle, excitement and expectation'. Bertie in Highland dress was not intimidated, but 'Vicky with very alarmed eyes making very low curtsies'.[25]

Although there were several private discussions about state business and the progress of the war, the Emperor and Empress had been thoughtful enough to bring a generous collection of presents for the children, as Affie recorded in his journal:

... to Vicky the Emperor gave a picture of a dog in tapestry – to Alice a peepshow which had some views of Paris in it, besides some very pretty landscapes. To Lenchen and Louise a large doll nearly as large as themselves, and a large box of games. To Arthur two tables full of soldiers – to Leopold two figures – a lady playing on a guitar – a doll which is wound up and moves its hands, and a Hussar and Vivandiere of his own regiments, which waltz and both run round the table and play; and to Bertie and me each a small cannon in imitation of the one which he invented himself.[26]

When the family found out – almost by accident – that the Emperor's birthday fell a day or two later, he was particularly touched when Arthur presented him with two violets, the flower of the Bonapartes.

In August 1855 the Queen, Prince Albert and the two eldest children accompanied their parents on a visit to Napoleon III's court at Paris. Vicky found the palace of Versailles breathtaking in its luxury, particularly as she had her own bedroom, from which a little door with white satin curtains opened on to a miniature garden scented with orange trees, and a splendid panoramic view of Paris greeted her gaze. At home, she always had to share a room with Alice.

Bertie, in a kilt, took the French by storm. His early experience of the French court was nothing short of a revelation, and he returned to England with his head full of the glittering imperial court, which made the entertainments at Buckingham Palace drab by comparison. He begged to be allowed to stay in Paris a little longer, asserting that he and his sister would not be missed, as 'there are six more of us at home'.

They were at Balmoral in September 1855 when they received the eagerly awaited news that Sebastopol was in the hands of the Allies, and there were celebrations, with the lighting of a bonfire, dancing to music provided by Her Majesty's piper, a veteran Highland soldier, and naturally several toasts in whisky. The children were allowed to share in the excitement, as the Queen recorded in her journal: 'The whole house seemed in a wonderful state of excitement. The boys were with difficulty awakened, and when at last this was the case, they begged leave to go up to the top of the cairn.'[27]

Four months later, Florence Nightingale was invited to Balmoral. Vicky had been allowed to read the newspapers, and studied the war reports eagerly. She asked about the fever, the cholera, cold and conditions generally, questions which Miss Nightingale answered plainly and directly. Prince Albert was much impressed with the interest his daughter was showing, way beyond her tender years.

In Victorian times, confirmation generally marked the end of childhood. Queen Victoria recorded the Princess Royal's confirmation on 20 March 1856, telling King Frederick William of Prussia that 'She has made her vow before the altar to follow the difficult road of life as a believing Christian.'[28]

In a sense, Vicky's childhood had come to an end some six months earlier. She was still only fourteen on 29 September 1855, when she became betrothed to the handsome Prince Frederick William of Prussia, 'Fritz' to the family. Her parents had not meant to announce the news until the time of her confirmation, though it leaked out almost at once, mainly through the indiscretion of her uncle Ernest, Duke of Coburg. In spite of this, the other children were not told until the following spring. Alice, 'who had no suspicion of such a thing, was told first,' the Queen wrote to Princess Augusta of Prussia, Fritz's mother (8 April 1856). 'She shows a touching love for her sister and tears come into her eyes when she speaks of it. Then the two boys and Lenchen were told. Bertie was particularly pleased about it and wrote to Fritz immediately. Alice will write to him today. *The missing Louise* and Arthur are to know nothing about it at present as they would not understand.'[29] One thing leads to another, and it was evident that the Queen did not wish natural curiosity to lead to uncomfortable questions too soon.

In the younger generation, there would be betrothal and marriage; in the older generation, death. The first family bereavement which affected the children at all was the passing of Queen Victoria's half-brother, Prince Charles of Leiningen. Though they hardly knew him, the elder ones were expected to take their part in the due solemnity of mourning. He was incapacitated after a severe stroke, news of which overshadowed Bertie's fifteenth birthday, as he recorded in a letter to Miss Hildyard (12 November 1856):

I thank you very much for the kind letter I received from you yesterday which I could not answer till today, I spent a very happy birthday, but unfortunately on account of dear Uncle Charles' illness nothing could be done, there was no 'feu-de-joie', no shooting or hunting, no dancing, or even musick [sic].

I fear every day we get worse news, and dear Mama has given up all hope for his recovery, it is very sad is it not, and just at this time for our two birthdays.[30]

Prince Charles died the following day, and court mourning doubtless made Vicky's birthday almost as gloomy as that of her brother.

On 14 April 1857 the Queen went into labour for the ninth and last time. A fifth daughter, christened Beatrice Mary Victoria Feodore, was born at 1.45 p.m.

'Mother and baby are well,' Prince Albert wrote to Princess Augusta of Prussia the following day. 'Baby practises her scales like a good *prima-donna* before a performance, and has a good voice! Victoria counts the hours and minutes like a prisoner. The children want to know what their sister is to be called, and dispute which names will sound best, and Vicky says with a sad sigh, "The little sister will never have known me in the house."'[31]

4

'Away from the happy peaceful home'

Princess Beatrice, the baby of Queen Victoria's family, remained 'Baby' in name for many years to come. She was christened Beatrice Mary Victoria Feodore in the chapel at Buckingham Palace on 16 June, with Vicky and Fritz among the godparents. As Vicky had remarked with sadness, she would never have the chance of knowing her youngest sister as well as the others, but once settled in Germany after her marriage she was kept informed in detail on the little girl's development and activities in the Queen's letters. One of the first great landmarks was her first birthday, when the Duchess of Kent came to breakfast, and the table was decorated with a giant 'B' in flowers, surrounded by candles. Gifts were piled high, among them Vicky's woolly lamb and a rose set in stones. Beatrice made it obvious that she preferred the lamb.

The differences between the Duchess of Kent and her daughter had long since faded into history. One of Prince Albert's first missions after marriage was to restore harmony between them, and soon the Queen – if she ever looked back to the old days – would rue how 'two people' (Conroy and Lehzen) had 'wickedly estranged us'. Grandmama indulged the children to her heart's content. It distressed her, she told the Queen, to hear a child being scolded and cry. 'Not when you have nine, Mamma!' was the brisk retort.

For the first four years, Beatrice enjoyed a privileged position. The rules which had kept the others in their place to a greater or lesser extent were relaxed for her. She was allowed to stay up late at night, come down and join her parents for dessert, and say virtually what she liked to her elders. 'Baby mustn't have that, it's not good for Baby,' the Queen would say at table as her daughter helped herself to food. 'But she likes it, my dear,'[1] was the three-year-old's reply, as she continued to help herself. 'I was very naughty last night,' she confessed when she was four. 'I would not speak to Papa, but it doesn't signify much.'[2] Another time, she was playing on the floor while the Queen was sitting at her desk writing. The nurse took her out, and in due course the Queen tried to get up from her chair – only to find that the little girl had taken advantage of her intense concentration on the letters by tying her securely by her apron strings. A maid had to be summoned to release her.[3]

Thoroughly spoilt, but good-natured and full of charm, nobody ever had the heart to scold her. Her father, created Prince Consort two months after her birth, was ageing beyond his years. Worn out by years of driving himself too hard, tired and careworn, it seemed at times that his youngest daughter was the only person who could bring him solace. He loved to sit her on his knee while he played the piano or organ, help her to sing nursery rhymes, and invite her to his dressing-room in the morning, watching him shave and feeding the little caged bird which he had taught to say 'Guten Morgen'. He read to her, taught her to draw, and strapped her on to Tommy, her first pony. The Queen noticed how the worry left her husband's face when he watched the little girl playing. As a result, she was showed more leniency and freedom from discipline than the others before her.

Although Beatrice only knew him for the first four years of her life, she never lost her German accent. Significantly, Queen Victoria never had more than a trace of it – noticeable, for instance, when she said 'tzo' instead of 'so'. Meeting Beatrice as a widow when she was in her seventies, the writer J.B. Priestley 'was astonished to discover what a thick German accent she had'.[4]

Beatrice was also something of a companion for the over-protected Leopold. Between his bouts of illness he was allowed to ride, join in amateur theatricals, and take part in country walks to hunt for geological specimens for the collection his father had encouraged him to make. Unfortunately, with his daring, strong-willed character, 'accidents' occurred, and he would have to rest in bed, a doctor in constant attendance. It was almost impossible to explain to him that his haemophilia prevented him from doing things which other boys could.

Arthur never gave his parents a moment's trouble. The Duke of Wellington's godson continued to give promise of wishing to follow a military career. There was often a military flavour to his presents. At Christmas 1855 he was given a replica of a Guards uniform, with bearskin hat and sword, as well as another box of lead soldiers to augment his collection of British army regiments. Once his elder sister was married, he began a collection of soldiers from Prussian regiments, and eagerly read up all he could about their history.

One morning, while he was still quite small, Arthur was taking his small terrier for a run in the grounds. A stable cat attacked the dog and threatened to maul it quite badly. Arthur came to the rescue, but was severely scratched in the process. On carrying the dog back to the house, his governess greeted him with horror. He explained the cause of his scratches briefly: 'Wounded in the execution of my duty!'[5]

When they were at Osborne, he was always happiest playing at the Royal Albert Barracks. The Prince Consort could recall having seen his uncle Leopold, now King of the Belgians, direct manoeuvres on the plains outside Brussels. He enjoyed helping Arthur to reconstruct these movements at the barracks with his growing collection of soldiers, and the boy would also enjoy devising his own battles and manoeuvres, lying on his stomach behind one of the miniature cannon standing at the four corners of the fort. Occasionally there were real-life battles of a less welcome sort, if an elder (and bigger) brother wanted to come and take charge, but very rarely. Bertie doubtless felt too grown-up to want to play such games with a brother eight years younger, while Affie was generally too occupied with maritime matters.

Without his beloved fort, at Balmoral Arthur found comfort in his imagination. Ancient struggles between the Picts and Scots could be readily conjured up mentally in the wild Deeside landscape, and in the evenings he could generally be found with his nose in a book, reading about the tribes, their feuds and conflicts. Sometimes he would try to reconstruct ancient skirmishes and battles, or work them out as true to the customs of those days as he could. With his vivid imagination, he was much quieter than the others, much better-behaved and less inclined to talk out of turn or try to attract his parents' attention. As a result, the Queen indulged him more than the others, especially when it came to small favours like being allowed to stay up late at Balmoral for a ghillies' dance.

In January 1859 the Prince Consort appointed Captain Elphinstone, an officer who had served in the Crimean war (and lost the sight of one eye during enemy action), as governor to Prince Arthur. That the Queen and Prince Consort had probably realized the excesses of the educational regime devised for Birch and Gibbs to carry out with the Prince of Wales is implicit from an entry in Elphinstone's diary in October 1858, while his appointment was being discussed. After lunching with the equerries and meeting Prince Arthur for the first time,

The Prince [Consort] then gave his views as regards education. 'How much may be learnt out of doors, by teaching a boy birds, the different plants, botany, geology, even the formation and variety of pebbles, it fixes the mind early. The time of learning ought to be regulated according to the capacity of the boy on that particular day, at times 3 hours or more would not distress, at other times one hour would be too much. That music had been too much forgotten with the elder Princes, that the Queen did not wish him to be taught too much at first, as he was still a boy, that one defect of private education is the want of emulation which stirs up the boy's energies; the only way that one can now adopt to make him do a thing would be to say that he ought to do it.'[6]

Admittedly, as a third son who was most unlikely to succeed to the British throne, or the duchy of Saxe-Coburg Gotha, Arthur's education was less important than those of his elder brothers. Nevertheless, their father's references to 'the capacity of the boy on that particular day', indicating a degree of licence not afforded to Bertie and Affie, suggest that he had modified his views.

Already Queen Victoria had privately admitted that Arthur was her favourite child. In a memorandum to her husband, also written in October 1858, she had spoken effusively of him: 'This Child is dear, *dearer* than any of the others put together, thus *after you* he is the *dearest* and *most precious* object to me on Earth.'[7]

Elphinstone may have found the parents rather more liberal with their third son than Birch and Gibbs had found them with Bertie, but his own duties were just as exacting. A large part of his work was taken up with tasks his daughter Mary (subsequently his biographer) described as 'the nursery-governess description', dealing not only with the routine of lessons, but also matters of discipline, health, and even clothing; hardly inspiring work for a military officer of twenty-eight. The Queen's letters, or rather written orders, to Elphinstone dealt with details such as eight to ten minutes being 'more than enough time for him to dress in', people to whom the Prince must write thank-you letters after his birthday, lists of what clothes and underclothes he was to wear, and the names and ages of boys whom he may have to play with in the afternoons.

As a treat Arthur was allowed the company of young Albert Grey, son of the Queen's secretary. Both apparently enjoyed playing Red Indians up and down the castle slopes. The sons of other members of the household, including young Lord Ely, whose mother was one of the Queen's ladies, were also allowed to join in his games.

Like the other tutors, Elphinstone recommended meeting boys at Eton – and on their own territory: 'mixing with boys of all kinds would "rub off" little eccentricities and softness of character which a home education must invariably produce. At the castle . . . other boys will give way to him and show him an amount of deference which must be injurious. This would not occur at Eton, where he meets boys on their own ground and where *he* is the stranger.'[8] This suggestion was apparently ignored.

The Prince Consort had a deep-seated opposition to public schools, which he regarded as 'barbarous, degrading and seminaries of vice'. In particular he deplored the idleness of cricket matches, in which an Etonian in the out-field could spend almost three hours doing nothing more strenuous than throwing the ball back if it came in his direction, or languidly sucking a blade of grass. When a plan was mooted to found a public school in honour of the Duke of Wellington, his first concern was that it 'should in *no way* become an Eton or Harrow.'[9]

Bertie was still studying under Gibbs, but his field of experience had been broadened somewhat. Gibbs had recommended a loosening of controls, such as travel, at home and abroad, which 'would remedy in some degree the disadvantages he labours from under a want of companions'.[10] On his fifteenth birthday, the Prince was allowed to choose his own food, his own ties, hats and similar trifles, but without any fixed allowance to pay for them. For all personal expenditure he remained dependent upon his parents.

That same autumn, 1856, he was allowed to go on a walking tour in Dorset, and the following year, with four boys of his own age hand-picked by the headmaster of Eton, and three tutors, he went on a walking tour of the Lake District. One of the boys, a year his senior, was William Henry Gladstone, elder son of the then Chancellor of the Exchequer and future Prime Minister.

It proved successful, and in July the Prince was sent on a study tour to Königswinter, near Bonn. The Prince Consort requested him to 'write to us a little more at length and give us your impressions of things, and not the mere bare facts'. Excursions were made into Switzerland and France, and the Prince was accompanied by his father's private secretary, General Charles Grey, Gibbs, and his father's equerry, Colonel Henry Ponsonby, who later became the Queen's private secretary after Grey's death. On the first evening after his arrival at Königswinter the Prince of Wales was treated to an excellent dinner, and presumably after a few glasses of wine, kissed a girl, and was scolded. William Gladstone described the incident in a letter to his mother, who told her husband. In reply, the latter called it 'this little squalid debauch', adding that it 'makes one feel what we should, I think, have suspected, viz. – that the Prince of Wales has not been educated up to his position. This sort of unworthy little indulgence is his compensation.'[11]

On his return home the Prince of Wales was given an annual allowance of £100, and granted permission to choose his own clothes, for which his parents would continue to pay. The Queen told him that neither she nor his father wanted 'to control your own tastes and fancies, which, on the contrary, we wish you to indulge and develop, but we do *expect* that you will never wear anything *extravagant* or *slang*, not because we don't like it, but because it would prove a want of self-respect and be an offence against decency, leading – as it has often done in others – to an indifference to what is morally wrong.'[12]

Although Bertie still gave cause for disappointment, Affie's excellent progress was some compensation. As a boy he was never bored, and could always be relied on to find something to interest him. It might be taking the dogs for a walk, or teaching them tricks; working at the carpenter's bench in the Swiss Cottage at Osborne, making a primitive musical box which played *Rule Britannia*, albeit after a fashion; or secretly learning to play the violin, as a surprise for his parents. Another lifelong passion had begun when he and Bertie were presented with a special advance sheet of the 6*d* lilac postage stamp on a visit in April 1856 to the official printers De La Rue in London. This was the start of the royal philatelic collection, destined to become the finest in the world – thanks largely to the boy's fascination with the infant hobby of philately.

When Affie was eleven, Prince Albert decided with misgivings that his sons would have to be separated. The difference in their ages and ability, he concluded, was a problem for both of them. Bertie was undoubtedly holding back, and perhaps influencing, his industrious younger brother. He did not want to hurt either of them, as both were mutually devoted, and he had never forgotten the pain of his parting from his brother Ernest, but for their own good it had to be done. Lieutenant John Cowell of the Royal Engineers, aged twenty-three, was chosen to superintend Affie's training for the Navy. He joined the royal household 'to learn the working of our system', and then took up quarters separately with Affie at Royal Lodge, Windsor Park. It proved too small and uncomfortable for the purpose, and they moved into larger premises at Alverbank, near Gosport. Affie studied under various tutors, learning geometry, mathematics, seamanship and navigation.

In August 1858 he sat his naval entrance examination, which he passed with very high marks. The Prince Consort was particularly proud, examining the written papers a few days later, to see that he solved the mathematical problems almost without any mistake, and did the translations without a dictionary. Lord Derby, the Prime Minister, commented obsequiously that he was grateful no such examination was necessary to qualify government ministers for office, 'as it would very seriously increase the difficulty of forming an administration.'[13]

There were no such problems for the parents when it came to the Princesses' education. Helena was happy left to her own devices. Not very artistic, though competent enough at music and copying drawings, and not interested in cooking in the Swiss cottage, she preferred being out in the open air. She would much rather help Affie in the workshop at Osborne, or play soldiers with Arthur in the fort. Horses were an abiding passion of hers, and she eagerly accepted the challenge of riding 'difficult' animals. She could calm a frightened or unmanageable horse, revealing a patience and sensitivity which she never did in the schoolroom. Queen Victoria was forever lamenting her unfeminine ways and lack of interest in her appearance, notably a readiness to get her hands dirty, and her love of food which made her put on weight. As far as Prince Albert was concerned, it did not matter in the slightest, and he readily encouraged her to spend as much time in the stables feeding and grooming the horses as she wanted.

Louise was only twenty-two months younger than Helena, and one might have expected a close bond to develop between them. It was not to be the case, for Louise, the child whom her mother had forecast at her birth would turn out to be 'something peculiar' was everything that Lenchen was not. 'That delicious baby Louise', as Lady Augusta Bruce called her, grew up to be the most attractive of the Princesses. She was never very practically minded, but extremely artistic, and had the temperament that went with it. She only joined in her sisters' activities with reluctance, and was skilled at baking scones and cakes in the Swiss Cottage kitchens, cutting out pastry with a teapot lid.

Yet she preferred her own company, painting and sketching. At the age of three she was given her first lessons in drawing and painting by Corbould, and it was evident that she was extraordinarily gifted. While her sisters might write stories for their own amusement, she would draw and paint landscapes from memory, or illustrate stories from a book that had been read to her. While they were generally happy to copy slavishly the well-known pictures that Corbould suggested, he taught her to use her originality, and to paint directly from nature. Charming little letters, essays and hand-painted cards framed in paper lace were regular presents to her father.

As the 'middle' sister, Louise often felt neglected. When Beatrice was born and became the apple of everyone's eye, she became jealous. Beatrice slept in the night nursery, and she felt excluded, with bad dreams and restless nights. When she was eleven, she gave Elphinstone 'such a pretty chair watch-stand' for his birthday, and when he tried to thank her she ran away shyly.

The wedding of Vicky and Fritz at St James's Palace on 25 January 1858 was an emotional occasion for all the children. The bride's brothers all wore Highland dress, while Alice, Louise and Helena were in pink satin trimmed with Newport lace, cornflowers and marguerites in their hair.

Surrounded by a family weeping with emotion, the bride and groom left Buckingham Palace on the morning of 2 February, braving the cold and snow in an open carriage, for Gravesend docks, where they were to sail across the North Sea to Germany. Only an hour after they left, the Queen sat down and wrote a long emotional letter in which she lamented her daughter's break with her childhood home; it was hard for parents to give up their children,

> and to see them go away from the happy peaceful home – where you used all to be around us! That is broken in, and you, though always our own dear child, and always able to be at home in your parents' house, are no longer one of the many, merry children who used to gather so fondly round us![14]

So began the voluminous mother–daughter correspondence which lasted until within a few weeks of the Queen's death, almost forty-three years later. To her unmarried sisters' regular instructions to bake for sick people in the neighbourhood in the kitchens at the Swiss Cottage was added a regular order 'for export'. Each week they cooked pies and cakes to send to Princess Frederick William of Prussia, taken by Queen's Messenger to Berlin, together with letters and other more conventional packages.

The elder children were growing up. As Vicky's childhood had ended officially with her confirmation in March 1856, so did Bertie's on 1 April 1858, although the nearest he came to adolescent emancipation was on his seventeenth birthday on 9 November that year. He received a rather portentous letter from his parents, informing him that he would be answerable in future not to his governor but to himself and his parents. His annual income was increased to £500, and he was told to free himself 'from the thraldom of abject dependence' upon servants, to learn to follow the precept of loving his neighbour as himself and to 'do unto men as you would they should do unto you', and to become a good man and a thorough gentleman. Life, he was warned (as if it was necessary to remind him), was 'composed of duties, and in the due, punctual and cheerful performance of them, the true Christian, true soldier and true gentleman is recognized.'[15] Much pleased and moved by the letter, apparently, he showed it to the Dean of Windsor and burst into tears.

On the following day Gibbs resigned his post at tutor. Not only Bertie was relieved to see him depart, with an annual pension of £800, the Order of Companion of the Bath and a lucrative practice on the Northern Circuit. To the Queen, the tutor had 'certainly failed during the last 2 years entirely, incredibly, and did Bertie no good'.[16] He was replaced by Colonel the Hon. Robert Bruce, brother of Lady Augusta, and a former Grenadier Guardsman, who was formally gazetted as the Prince of Wales's governor.

It had been a year of one upheaval after another. Soon after passing his naval entrance examination, fourteen-year-old Affie went to sea. Bitterly, the Queen told Vicky after his departure that 'it is much better to have no children than to have them only to give them up!'[17]

By this time, the Queen was looking forward – with very mixed feelings – to being a grandmother. Vicky was expecting her first child, but not all her brothers and sisters were allowed to share the news. Not even twelve-year-old Lenchen was to know, as the Queen said (27 October): 'those things are not proper to be told to children, as it initiates them into things which they ought not to know of, till they are older.'[18] The news was broken to the children in January 1859 that, in the triumphant words of Louise, they were no longer mere royal children, 'we are uncles and aunts'. Sometimes lacking in over-confidence, and keen for attention, Louise tended to react with over-enthusiasm. That Princess Frederick William of Prussia had had a dangerous confinement in which both mother and baby would have died but for the timely intervention of a Scottish doctor who helped them when the German doctors had given up hope, and that the baby Prince William was left with a withered left arm, was not revealed to the young uncles and aunts for some time.

Despite her gruesome first experience of childbirth, the Princess had seven more children during the next thirteen years. In July 1860 she produced a daughter, named Charlotte. To celebrate, the uncles and aunts at Osborne were allowed a half holiday and spent it cooking in the Swiss Cottage. The Prince Consort used the opportunity to explain the facts of life to Alice, and at Osborne healths were drunk to the new child, who arrived in the world with none of the complications or horrors that had beset her elder brother's birth. With a touch of his old humour which was seen but rarely by now, the Prince Consort wrote to Vicky to suggest that the baby should model herself on her aunt Beatrice. The latter, aged only three, would readily excuse herself from less congenial tasks, saying that she had no time because she must write letters to her niece.

Alice was confirmed in April 1859, a couple of days before her sixteenth birthday. To mark this transition to adult life, she was presented with a large quantity of jewellery, including a diamond necklace and earrings. Her matrimonial future was already under review, though her self-confidence was not helped when her first prospective suitor, the Prince of Orange, was invited to a dinner-party at Buckingham Palace and put himself out of the running by his boorish behaviour towards her. A few months later Prince Louis of Hesse and the Rhine, heir presumptive to the dukedom, was chosen. An unintelligent man whose manners and morals were, however, beyond reproach, he was warmly endorsed by the Queen and Prince Consort, and they were betrothed in November 1860.

The youngest children were coming to an age when they could benefit from their father's close interest and encouragement. It goes without saying that he was gratified by the developing artistic skills of Louise and the precocious intellect of Leopold, while Arthur's dedication to military interest was a similar source of pleasure.

Yet 1861 was to be a tragic year for the whole family. The Duchess of Kent was suffering from erysipelas, and by the beginning of the year her life was despaired of. She died on 16 March, aged seventy-four, and the grief-stricken Queen verged on a nervous breakdown for several months. Beatrice touched her mother when she spoke continually of Grandmama, 'how she is in heaven, but hopes she will return'.[19]

It increased the burdens on the Prince Consort. Unrecognized by the family, he was chronically sick and, as he admitted, he would not struggle against severe illness but give up at once. At the end of November he caught a severe chill, and a few days later he retired to his bed.

Alice took on herself much of the duty of nursing him. He asked her if she had told Vicky in Berlin – recovering from a severe bout of pneumonia, expecting a third child, and not deemed well enough to make the journey – that he was ill. Alice told him that she had. He replied with resignation, 'You should have told her I was dying.' The doctors, including Sir James Clark, who was scornfully pronounced by some of his contemporaries as not fit to tend a sick cat, seemed unprepared to admit to the Queen how little hope there was.

On the afternoon and evening of 14 December, as he lay in bed at Windsor Castle, most of the children who were present were brought in for a last look at him. Apart from Vicky, Affie (at sea), Leopold (who had been sent with a governor to convalesce from measles in the south of France) and Louise and Beatrice (considered too young), they all came to take their last fond farewell of him. Arthur was brought in and escorted out, white with horror. The Prince of Wales, Alice and Helena were among the company kneeling round the bed when he passed away at 10.50 that evening.

Temporarily numb with shock as she was helped out of the room, it is said, the Queen visited the nursery, took Beatrice out of her cot without waking her and held her in her arms. The so-called eyewitness accounts of Queen Victoria's actions in the first two or three hours of her widowhood are often at variance with one another, but if this one is true, it was a most symbolic gesture.

Louise was only told the following morning. 'Oh, why did not God take me. I am so stupid and useless,'[20] was her lament.

The Queen and her daughters withdrew to Osborne early the following week, while the male members of the family represented them at the Prince Consort's funeral on 23 December at St George's Chapel, Windsor. It was noted by a reporter that the Prince of Wales 'bore up bravely . . . but his closely-drawn lips, and from time to time a convulsive twitching of the shoulders, showed how much he was enduring'. The Duke of Saxe-Coburg and Prince Louis of Hesse were less restrained in their emotion, while ten-year-old Arthur, 'in a black dress of Highland fashion, walked by his brother's side, and the poor little boy sobbed and wept as though his heart would break. It is good for children to weep thus.'[21]

Mrs Thurston described the deathbed scene to her daughter, Elizabeth Bryan (24 December):

> I will try to answer your questions respecting the last hours of our ever to be lamented Prince Consort, but as he was unconscious nearly all Friday & Saturday I do not think he knew any of those around him altho the Queen & Princess Alice both feel, he knew them nearly at the last – I hear he scarcely moved, but remained, with his eyes closed, when his dear children were taken in, each separately, by Sir Jas Clarke & the Princess Leiningen – he did not speak to either of them, dear little Beatrice had not seen him for many days previous to his death. (& I feel astonished she does not speak more of him).[22]

Perhaps Beatrice had inferred from her mother that it was as well not to ask when Papa was coming home. Only gradually did it dawn on the girl of four that she would never see him again. Even Vicky, who came to England three months later, once she was considered well enough to make the journey, heartbroken at the loss of the father to whom she had perhaps been closer than anybody else, was preoccupied primarily with trying to help her mother find the resolution to 'still endure', and thought that her youngest sister was too young to understand. The little girl who had been so cheerful became quiet and withdrawn. Her childish giggle was heard less, and the comical sayings which had so delighted the grown-ups tailed off.

The Queen confessed that she was almost totally dependent on Beatrice. When Vicky wrote to send her good wishes for her youngest sister's fifth birthday, the Queen referred to her as 'the only thing that keeps me alive, for she alone wants me really'.[23]

The artistic Louise, only thirteen years old, produced a series of haunting tributes in watercolour to her father. The first, painted for the Queen's wedding anniversary in February, portrayed a sleeping figure in bed – presumably the Queen herself – and, in an ethereal haze above, a vision of her reunion with the Prince

Consort. Three months later, she presented the Queen on her birthday with another bedside scene in which she was accompanied by two of her daughters, while a group of three angels looked down on them. The whole was inscribed 'Blessed are they that mourn, For they shall be comforted.' For the first anniversary of her father's death, Louise painted a picture of Mary Magdalen and an angel outside the open tomb. Such pictures, which were presumably in the nature of set pieces suggested by Corbould, helped to soothe the Queen in the first months of her overwhelming grief.

Princess Alice's wedding on 1 July was held in the dining-room at Osborne, converted into a temporary chapel for the purpose. Helena, Louise and Beatrice were among the bridesmaids at the little ceremony which, the Queen admitted, was more like a funeral than a wedding. Affie sobbed bitterly throughout the service, and after the bride and groom left, Arthur solemnly announced that when he married, 'I shall bring my wife home to live with us all, and we shall eat our own cake.'[24] Maybe he had taken the Queen's mournful words about Alice going to make her home in Germany to heart; at any rate, he must have deplored the absence of wedding cake.

5

'Dreadfully wild, but I was just as bad'

A new generation of royal children was growing up at court, overlapping with the old. Princess Beatrice was twenty-one months old when she became an aunt in January 1859 with the birth of Prince William of Prussia. On one of his early visits to England, the boy was most amused to find that his little aunt was called 'baby' by the family. Affronted at his copying them, she told him firmly that he must call her aunt. Time after time he refused, before giving in with bad grace. 'Aunt *Baby* then!'

When he attended the wedding of his uncle Bertie to Princess Alexandra ('Alix') of Denmark, on 10 March 1863, he soon became bored. His uncles Arthur and Leopold, like him clad in Highland dress, had been put in charge of him. When he got the cairngorm out of the head of his dirk and threw it across the floor, his small uncles remonstrated, whereupon he bit them in the legs. In view of Leopold's haemophilia, such behaviour could have been dangerous, but as Leopold showed no ill-effects the 'bite' was obviously not very deep.

At the same time Beatrice made an interesting, if slightly alarming discovery while being taken for a ride round Windsor. Turning to Lady Augusta Bruce, she exclaimed in a shocked tone of voice, 'Guska, I *never* thought there was *stays* in shops.'[1] On the subject of her brother's wedding, she had evidently learnt from her mother that such occasions were not to be regarded as a subject for rejoicing. She did not like weddings, she said, and would never get married herself. She would stay with Mama.

At the time of her brother's wedding, Alice was eight months pregnant. Denied the chance to be with Vicky at any of her confinements or even christenings, Queen Victoria was determined that with her second daughter it should be different. On 5 April Alice gave birth to a daughter, appropriately named Victoria. Their sister's 'interesting' condition was a source of wonder to Helena and Louise who were still considered not old enough to know, although they may have guessed something of the sort when their mother was growing large before the appearance of Beatrice. It has been suggested that they were vaguely aware of their mother's jealousy of Alice's condition, that she could not have another child herself, and that to some extent this new grandchild was a child-substitute.

Princess Victoria of Hesse and Prince William of Prussia were always among the Queen's favourite grandchildren, although the latter – in childhood as well as in imperial splendour, thirty years hence – was notorious for his mischievous behaviour. When William Powell Frith was painting his officially commissioned portrait of the Prince and Princess of Wales's wedding later that year at Windsor Castle, the four-year-old Prince gave him endless trouble. 'Mr Fiff,' he told the artist, 'you are a nice man, but your whiskers –'. Helena immediately came and put a firm hand over his mouth. Struggling free, he repeated himself more loudly, 'Your whiskers –'. His aunt stopped him again, blushing but unable to stop herself laughing. She led him to the other side of the studio and gave him a gentle lecture on good manners.

'The little imp', as Frith called him, was fascinated by watching the picture of 'Uncle Wales's wedding' gradually taking shape. In an attempt to keep him quiet Frith allowed him to paint a small picture on one corner of the canvas, about a foot square. All was peaceful for some time, until the nurse came in and caught sight of the boy. 'Look at his face!' she exclaimed in horror. 'What has he been doing to it?' He had been wiping his brushes on it, richly decorating himself with uneven streaks of bright colour. Assuring her that he could easily remedy the situation, Frith grabbed him with one hand and rubbed turpentine into his face with the other. A small amount got into a scratch on the Prince's skin, and he screamed as he struck the artist as hard as his fist would allow. Bellowing 'You nasty Mr Fiff!', he hid under the table and shrieked until he was exhausted. For the rest of his stay at Windsor that month, he took his revenge on Frith by sitting so badly that the latter failed to produce anything more than a vague likeness.[2]

By this time Prince Arthur was living at the Ranger's House, Blackheath. The idea had evidently been either that of the Prince Consort, or had received his sanction, otherwise Elphinstone would have almost certainly found it impossible to put into effect in the face of the Queen's somewhat grudging assent. The governor had seen with concern not only the harmful effect that isolated life at court would have on the boy's character, but also how wrong it was for the child to remain in such an atmosphere of gloom. In the autumn of 1862, with Elphinstone as comptroller, Mr Jolley as tutor, and Mr Collins as valet, Arthur settled into his new home just inside Greenwich Park. This remained the Prince's headquarters for nearly nine years, until the summer of 1871, when he was twenty-one. Apart from a year's military service in Canada at the age of nineteen, and occasional visits elsewhere in England and to Europe, he stayed mainly at Blackheath. There were regular breaks at Balmoral, Osborne and Windsor at birthdays and Christmas, but in view of the Queen's prolonged mourning, these must have been duty visits rather than occasions of great enjoyment.

One of the first letters written by Elphinstone after their arrival assured Her Majesty that every room had a thermometer, and he would personally see that a temperature of 60°F was never exceeded; and he would report on his charge's progress every Tuesday, Thursday and Saturday.[3]

Elphinstone took his duties conscientiously, as indeed he needed to. In theory it was his duty to write three times a week to the Queen, reporting in detail on Prince Arthur's doings. In practice he wrote far more often than this. If they were travelling, or if the Prince was ill, letters might be sent to the Queen twice a day, often written long after midnight.

The Queen stressed that her son's natural kindliness must not be spoiled by selfishness or cynicism; he must always put the welfare of others before his own, and realize that as a prince his life would not be one of mere pleasure but of service to his country. She was afraid that, living so much away from home, 'he should become a *stranger* to that sad and fatherless home and be as *reserved* as alas, for the last 6 or 7 years our elder sons have been and still are'.[4]

Elphinstone was quick to reassure her that this would not be the case, and that being at Greenwich would not increase the boy's self-importance as much as being at court, where deference and admiration were shown to him daily if not hourly: 'Here on the contrary he walks about without being taken notice of, frequently jostled by workmen returning to their work.'[5]

Pocket money was not unlimited. One Christmas he wanted to give Louise a rather special present. Two teeth of a stag he had shot were sent to Garrard the jewellers, to be mounted into a butterfly-shaped brooch. 'He had been told at Balmoral that the expense of so doing would not exceed what he could afford out of his very small allowance of pocket money. It is unnecessary to state that the allowance is not sufficient to cover the expense, although very little in itself.'[6]

Living in London meant it was possible for Prince Arthur and Elphinstone to visit museums and exhibitions on a regular basis. The Crystal Palace had just been removed from its original home in Hyde Park to Sydenham, not far from Greenwich, and many afternoons were spent there.

It was not a case of 'all work and no play'. The Prince found a merry-go-round and begged his comptroller to be allowed to try it. After hesitating, and deciding that nobody would recognize the Prince, Elphinstone reluctantly gave his approval. In telling the Queen, he remarked a little cravenly that 'he thought Your Majesty would not object, the circumstance not being likely to occur again'. He worried too much, for the Queen assured him she was '*much* rejoiced that our dear little Darling was so much amused at the Crystal Palace, as she knows how much the beloved Prince would rejoice at his dear children being happy'.[7]

This was the age of the London fair with, in the words of Arthur Bryant, 'its rows of booths hung with dolls, gilt gingerbreads and brandy balls, its raree-shows and performing pigs, its giants and its dwarfs,' where apprentices and boys 'pushed about with whistles, penny trumpets, false noses and rolled twopenny scrapers . . . down the backs of their elders';[8] while the park was filled with youngsters playing traditional games like kiss-in-the-ring, riding donkeys, or turning somersaults down the hill. Prince Arthur, it may be assumed, would have been 'much amused' at these sights, even if Queen Victoria might have frowned on him doing much more than observing them at a safe distance.

As in the case of his two elder brothers, Arthur suffered from the lack of suitable companions. Elphinstone was concerned that acquaintance with a small number of boys would 'create a closer intimacy than might be advisable at Prince Arthur's present age unless one is *perfectly* acquainted with the character of the boys'.[9] Nevertheless there were games of football with Mr Jolley and some of the servants, 'most respectable men from whom . . . no harm could be learnt'. Instructors from Woolwich taught him fencing and gymnastics, riding and jumping over fences in the park, and in winter, games of hockey on the ice.

Reading did not apparently play a major part in this active Prince's upbringing, but he seems to have enjoyed travel books. Religion was an important element, but not merely a question of Sunday observance. When the Queen heard that he was being given religious lessons on a Sunday, she objected; once the children were old enough to go to church, she stipulated, religious lessons on the same day should be avoided. Perhaps once a week (on weekdays), the ancient history lesson could be devoted to religion instead. Sunday morning service was always attended, prayers being read at home if illness prevented him from going.

In July 1866, at the age of sixteen, he was sent to Woolwich to begin his military training. The Queen insisted that he should still live at the Ranger's House, and not in the barracks. In every other way, she maintained, he was to be treated like an ordinary officer. His 'purity', she was convinced, would protect him from sin; but she did not wish to take the risk of giving him too much freedom, as she had his elder brothers – who had wasted little time in succumbing to the pleasures of the flesh which had come their (not unwilling) way.

By midsummer 1863 the Princess of Wales was expecting a child. Bertie and Alix had thrown themselves into the round of social life in London with a readiness that led Queen Victoria to criticize their going out every night 'till she will become a skeleton, and hopes there cannot be!' Yet hopes there were before long, and the child was expected in March or April 1864.

As there was still much decorating to be done at Sandringham, the estate purchased for them in Norfolk, the Prince and Princess of Wales spent Christmas at Frogmore House, the former home of the Duchess of Kent. A severe frost made conditions ideal for skating on Frogmore Lake. As Alix's condition made participation in the sport inadvisable, she had to content herself with watching her husband and friends from the comfort of a sledge-chair on the ice. Though she had been suffering some twinges of pain on the afternoon of 8 January 1864, she was determined not to be left indoors. Only after they returned to the house at dusk did Lady Macclesfield, her lady-in-waiting and the mother of thirteen children, realize that the birth was imminent. At nine o'clock that evening she gave birth to a son weighing three and three-quarter pounds. Although small, he appeared to be well.

Second in line to the throne, he was named Albert Victor, after the Queen and the Prince Consort. The parents were obliged to accept the Queen's decision, though the Prince made plain his annoyance to her when Beatrice told Lady Macclesfield that Mama had settled what the names were to be before he had had a chance to speak to her about it. In order that they should have some choice themselves, the supplementary names Christian Edward, after the baby's maternal grandfather and father, were added. Grandpapa's presence was also felt at the baptism on 10 March. A chorale by the Prince Consort, 'Praise the Lord with heart and voice', with words by Thomas Oliphant, was sung at the Queen's request.

In spite of her oft-expressed aversion to the frog-like physical characteristics of tiny babies, Queen Victoria was strangely complimentary about 'Eddy', her first grandson to be born on British soil. At the age of ten weeks, she remarked on his 'well-shaped head and a great look of dear Alix', and called him 'a very pretty, but rather a fidgety baby'.[10]

That she should have the ultimate say in the baby's upbringing, and that of any Wales children which might follow, the Queen made plain in a letter to King Leopold (11 March 1864); her eldest son 'should understand what a strong right I have to interfere in the management of the child or children; that he should never do anything about the child without consulting me'.[11]

On 3 June 1865 the Princess had a second son, whom they named George, but always 'Georgy' in the family. During her third pregnancy she became seriously ill with rheumatic pains and fever, which failed to abate even after the birth of a daughter, Louise, on 20 February 1867. It was over two months before she could be wheeled to her bedroom window for a sight of the spring weather, and she was still wheelchair-bound on 10 May when the Princess was christened. The fever left her permanently lame and exacerbated her tendency to hereditary deafness. Two more daughters followed at almost symmetrical intervals, Victoria in July 1868 and Maud in November 1869. Eddy and Louise were sickly, delicate infants, but the others throve.

The same could not be said for their third son and last child, born on 6 April 1871 and hastily christened Alexander John Charles Albert shortly before his death at the age of twenty-four hours. Queen Victoria was fortunate in that all her children, even the frail Leopold, lived to maturity. Her eldest son was not so lucky. The Prince of Wales had not made himself popular during the last few years by his endless pursuit of pleasure while his wife was lying ill at home, particularly around the time of Princess Louise's birth, when her rheumatic fever was at its most serious. He had shown the tendency common to immature adults to shut his eyes to anything frightening or unpleasant; it was made plain to him by their household that if he sat around in the sickroom he was in the way, and he was easily bored.

But at the death of this frail little infant, the lady-in-waiting, Mrs Stonor, was taken aback to see him, the tears rolling down his cheeks, insisting on putting the tiny body into a coffin himself and carefully arranging the white satin pall and the little bouquets of white flowers. The Princess was not well enough to leave the house, and from her bedroom window she watched her husband walking in the short funeral procession hand-in-hand with Eddy and Georgy, dressed for mourning in grey kilts, crepe scarves and black gloves.

As parents the Prince and Princess of Wales followed a very different regime, a world away from the pedantic rules of Baron Stockmar and Prince Albert which had blighted the heir to the throne's adolescent days. The Princess had been brought up in a comparatively informal atmosphere in Copenhagen, where she was one of a relatively poor but happy family of six children. At the time of her birth, her father, Prince Christian, had not expected to ascend the throne of Denmark (which he did in November 1863, eight months after her wedding). The Danish Princes and Princesses had been an extroverted, high-spirited crowd, with little in the way of intellectual leanings. They became good linguists, learning French and German; they had English nurses, and English became a second language. Prince Christian taught them gymnastics and physical education, while Princess Christian taught them domestic science, religion and music, but in other aspects their educational regime was a relaxed one. It was to such an upbringing that Princess Alexandra looked to for a model when helping to raise her children, a principle with which her husband was in full agreement – as far as the Queen would permit.

The Wales children enjoyed a happy, carefree country childhood spent mostly on the Sandringham estate in Norfolk. They rode ponies, looked after pets, and learnt the names of birds and wild flowers in the countryside. The Prince of Wales's household moved from their London home, Marlborough House, to Osborne Cottage immediately after the London season and before the Cowes regatta. In mid-August they joined the Queen on the Balmoral estate, at Abergeldie, and returned to Norfolk in the autumn. Christmas was always spent at Sandringham.

Sometimes there were visits to society friends of the Prince and Princess of Wales. The latter wrote to the Duchess of Sutherland (21 June 1866) from Marlborough House:

As you were kind enough the other day to ask me to bring our eldest little boy with us to Trentham, and I now come to ask if you really have a little place to spare for him as now we shall be delighted to bring him. If it is possible to find a little corner near our rooms I shall be still more thankful as I shall only take the Nursery maid with us – My maid's room, I mean she had one the last time we were at Trentham, would do beautifully for him, and my two maids might go anywhere together!! I hope this won't be very inconvenient to you dear Duchess, but as you were too kind the other day yourself to propose our taking the little one with us, I therefore come to ask you if there still was room for him.[12]

The boys were always devoted to each other, though the difference in their characters was readily discernible. Eddy took after their mother; taller, diffident, lethargic, lacking a healthy complexion, he was her favourite. Georgy was stronger and more high-spirited. Amusing, inquisitive and hot-tempered, he took the initiative in childhood pranks, and showed himself a born leader in the nursery. Though inclined to be shy, he had an easy-going manner, and was naturally neat and orderly. Close observers thought him very like his father at a similar age – but with the difference that Georgy did not suffer from having another Stockmar to look over his shoulder and bemoan his failings.

With Queen Victoria's children, there were several governesses, servants and relations ready to record countless anecdotes of the youngsters, as well as the Queen's and Prince Albert's letters and journals. No such detailed documentation of the young Wales's formative days has been passed on. However the story has persisted that Georgy was scolded by his grandmother at lunch one day for behaving like an animal. She sent him under the table as a punishment, it is said, and he emerged a few minutes later without any clothes on.*

Annie de Rothschild met the children on a visit to Holkham in December 1869, and commented to her mother that 'the two little boys toddled in first with great self-possession'. They were 'very nice little boys, rather wild, but not showing signs of becoming too much spoiled; they make very ludicrous attempts at being dignified.' She taught them blind man's buff, and ran races with them. They were evidently very high-spirited and perhaps not on their best behaviour. The Princess of Wales told her with an apologetic smile, 'They are dreadfully wild, but I was just as bad.'[13]

Queen Victoria's attitude to the children was one of indulgence tempered with exasperation. They could be 'very amusing' or 'very merry in my room' if she was in a good mood, or 'such ill-bred, ill-trained children I can't fancy them at all'.[14] They were certainly not as healthy as she would have wished; when Princess Victoria was six months old, she commented in despair to the Crown Princess of Prussia that they were 'most wretched, excepting Georgie, who is always merry and rosy'.[15] The Queen frequently disagreed with her

---

* The same story has been told about the Queen's eldest grandchild, Prince William of Prussia. It is more likely to relate to Prince George. With his deformed left arm, William would have had great difficulty in taking off his clothes unaided.

daughter-in-law on the way they brought up their children, but the Queen readily admitted that 'One thing, however, she does insist on, and that is great simplicity and an absence of all pride, and in that respect she has my fullest support.'[16]

In April 1870 Robert Collins, a much-respected royal servant of several years' standing, was playing games with the Princes. In their excitement, George kicked him on the shin. 'Don't do that again,' Mr Collins ordered him sharply. The Prince promptly did. For his defiance Mr Collins turned him over and spanked him twice. The boy went very red but did not cry, and in a minute the game resumed. But he had learnt his lesson, and there was no defiance in future.

The children's main playmates were their Teck cousins. The children of Francis, Duke of Teck and his wife Mary Adelaide, sister of the Duke of Cambridge, were Victoria Mary (born in 1867), Adolphus (1868), Francis (1870), and Alexander (1874). They lived at White Lodge, Richmond, and Kensington Palace. The children would meet regularly to play at one or other of the London homes during the summer, or at Chiswick House, lent to the Prince and Princess of Wales by the Duke of Devonshire.

There are references to the children of both families playing happily among the sphinxes and the obelisks, and in the small temple by the lake at Chiswick House. The girls played with the Wales's rickety old dolls and battered toys, probably handed down from the Princess of Wales's spartan Copenhagen childhood. Meanwhile the boys would amuse themselves by the lakeside, throwing stones in the water or having races with the small wooden boats carved for them by the Chiswick footmen. Tea was taken with their nurses, who 'treated them without ceremony'.

When staying at Osborne, the boys would play – but not too vigorously – with their uncle Leopold. Unhappily, every time he fell he brought on an attack of internal bleeding, which meant a spell in bed. The boys soon learnt to be careful when he was around. It was frustrating for him, who was very fond of his nephews and always ready to join in their games. He was equally devoted to his sister-in-law, who was the only member of the family who could influence him in his stubborn moods. As she suffered so early in life from lameness and deafness, she could sympathize with him in his physical afflictions and realize what it meant not to be allowed to lead a 'normal' life.

When Eddy was a fortnight old, a personal attendant, or 'nursery footman', Charles Fuller, was appointed to look after him. He served both Princes, and after his retirement wrote to them regularly until his death in 1901.

By the time he was six years of age, the high-spirited Georgy was starting to dominate his brother. This tendency, it was hoped, would be kept in check by the appointment of a tutor. The choice fell on John Neale Dalton, son of the vicar of Milton Keynes. A bachelor of thirty-two, he had taken first-class honours in theology at Cambridge, followed by Holy Orders. At the time of his appointment he was curate to Canon Prothero at Whippingham Church, a post for which his notoriously loud booming voice made him well qualified. His candidature as the Princes' tutor was doubtless endorsed by the Canon, a close friend and regular confidante of the Queen when she was at Osborne. He joined the Wales's household in 1871 and stayed with them for fourteen years, and soon gained the boys' affection and respect.

Every detail of the Princes' education was discussed by the Prince of Wales and Dalton. The memories of his own youth were vivid and sometimes bitter, and the Prince was determined that there should be no repetition where his sons were concerned. The important principle, they were agreed, was that the boys' childhood should be happy. Hard work and a general education on lines as liberal as circumstances permitted were next in importance, and as far as possible they should be treated as ordinary boys. Such a request, made by royal parents of every generation, was almost impossible to comply with, but in this case there was one marked departure from the dictum of Queen Victoria and the Prince Consort. Princes Albert Victor and George, their father insisted, were never to be denied the companionship of children of their own age.

Dalton evidently spared little effort to win their trust. In his later years King George V would stop to point out the spot in the grounds of Sandringham where the tutor used to teach them to shoot with bow and arrow, and a certain spot when he let them shoot at him as the running deer. He inculcated in both boys the value and duty of daily prayer and Bible reading, reinforcing the principles they had already learnt from their mother who used to read aloud to them from the scriptures. His efforts to interest them in art and architecture were less successful. Visits to monuments and shrines, churches and galleries in London, struck little chord in them.

It was his practice to combine business with pleasure, instruction with recreation, while keeping them hard at work. In this he proved more successful than Mr Gibbs, although neither of the Princes were scholastically or intellectually inclined.

Dalton's timetable required the boys to rise at 7 a.m., studying geography and English before breakfast. At 8 a.m. they had a Bible or history lesson, followed at 9 a.m. by algebra or Euclid. An hour's break for games came next, followed by French or Latin until the main meal at 2 p.m. The afternoon was set aside for games, usually cricket, or riding, then tea, followed by English lessons, music and preparation. Bedtime was at 8 p.m.

Regular reports on their progress were sent to Queen Victoria. Writing from Sandringham (31 January 1874), he reported to her:

Prince Albert Victor and Prince George of Wales are both in the enjoyment of the most thorough good health and spirits, and also daily prosecute their studies with due diligence and attention. Their Royal Highnesses live a very regular and quiet life in the country here, and keep early hours both as to rising in the morning and retiring to rest at night. . . . The two little Princes ride on ponies for an hour each alternate morning in the week; and take a walk on the other three days, in the afternoon also their Royal Highnesses take exercise on foot. As regards the studies, the writing, reading, and arithmetic are all progressing favourably; the music, spelling, English history, Latin, geography, and French all occupy a due share of their Royal Highnesses' attention, and progress in English history, and geography is very marked.[17]

Dalton kept two large albums which he used to record their proficiency in all subjects of the curriculum. Every Saturday he added general remarks on their conduct during the week. Prince George was not free from the same faults which had troubled his father at a similar age. When he was eleven, it was noted that one week he had 'been much troubled by silly fretfulness of temper and general spirit of contradiction', despite which his work was 'up to the usual average'. A few months later, Dalton wrote, the Prince needed 'steady application. Though he is not deficient in a wish to progress, still his sense of self-approbation is almost the only motive power in him. He has not nearly so high a sense of right and wrong for its own sake as his elder brother.'[18]

The boy must have been heartily thankful that his father took such comments less seriously than his late grandfather would have done, though when he became a father himself, Prince George would view tutors' reports on his own offspring as gravely as any parent of the Victorian age.

Princess Victoria aged eleven, from a painting by Richard Westall, her drawing master, 1830. Although the likeness of its subject is good, the woodland landscape setting reveals a degree of artistic licence. It is unlikely that the closely supervised Princess would ever have been allowed outside sketching in such a casual manner

Group of small dolls, with dresses made by Princess Victoria and Baroness Lehzen between 1830 and 1833, representing ballet and opera performers seen on stage in London

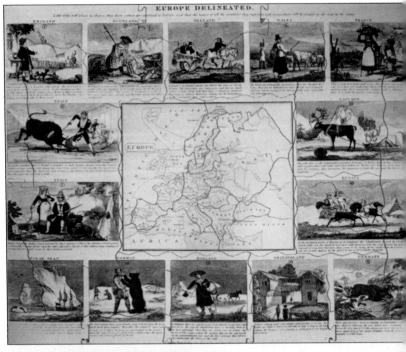

'Europe Delineated', a dissected puzzle comprising fifty-seven pieces cut from a hand-coloured steel engraving mounted on wood, by John Betts, *c.* 1830. When fully assembled, the map could be used as a race game. One of the most popular games of its type, it was probably used by Princess Victoria in her geography lessons and handed down to her second cousin Princess Victoria Mary of Teck, later Queen Mary, who played with it as a child and presented it to the Museum of Childhood, Bethnal Green, in 1936

Princess Victoria rescued from a falling mast on board the yacht *Emerald*, while sailing from Torquay to Plymouth, 2 August 1833

The christening of the Princess Royal, commemorative plate

The christening of Victoria, Princess Royal, at Buckingham Palace, 10 February 1841, engraving after a portrait by Charles Robert Leslie. Figures include, from left: Mary, Duchess of Gloucester; the Duchess of Kent; Leopold, King of the Belgians; Augustus, Duke of Sussex (in skull cap); Queen Adelaide, facing the Archbishop of Canterbury. Queen Victoria and Prince Albert are on the right

Victoria, Princess Royal, with Eos, Prince Albert's favourite greyhound, engraving after a portrait by Edwin Landseer, 1841

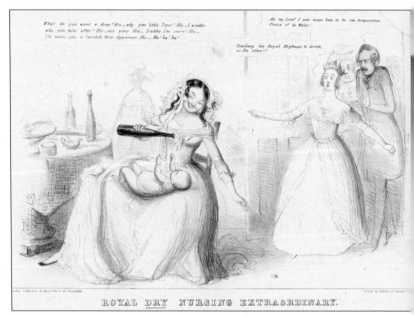

'Royal Dry Nursing Extraordinary', from a cartoon, *c.* 1842

Princess Alice with Eos, engraving after a painting by Edwin Landseer, 1843

The Duchess of Kent, Queen Victoria and Prince Albert with the children at Christmas, 1848

The royal children with their nurse, Mrs Mary Ann Thurston. Left to right: the Prince of Wales, Princess Helena, Princess Alice (in front), the Princess Royal, Prince Alfred, Princess Louise (in Mrs Thurston's arms). Photograph by William Kilburn, 22 June 1848

Prince Alfred and Princess Helena, engraving after a painting by Franz Xavier Winterhalter, 1849

Osborne House

The Swiss cottage, Osborne House

The royal children in *Athalie*, 1853, engraving after a drawing by Queen Victoria. The cast also included children from two other families at court, the Phipps and the Seymours

The royal children in *Die Tafelbirnen*, 1853, engraving after a drawing by Queen Victoria. Left to right: Conrad (Helena), Annette (Alice), Albert (Alfred), Minna (Louise), Max (Prince of Wales), Louise (Princess Royal

Prince Arthur, after a drawing by Franz Xavier Winterhalter, *c.* 1855

The Field of Battle, watercolour by Victoria, Princess Royal, 1855

Princess Beatrice, 1860

Prince Leopold and Prince Arthur, 1860

Prince William of Prussia at the age of eighteen months, sketched by Queen Victoria at Coburg, August 1860

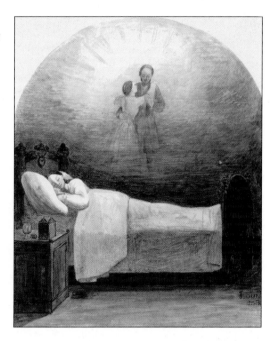

Memorial picture, painted by Princess Louise, February 1862, for her parents' twenty-second wedding anniversary – which the Prince Consort did not live to see

Prince Leopold with his dogs Curran, Waldmann and Comet, in the garden at Windsor, April 1865. Photograph by Prince Alfred, the first member of the royal family to master the art of the camera

The nursery bedroom, Osborne, photograph by Jabez Hughes, *c.* 1873. The swing cradle with mahogany frame (centre) was made for the Princess Royal in 1840; the bed (right) was slept in by a nurse

The Edinburgh children, 1881. From left: Princess Marie, Princess Victoria Melita, Princess Alexandra, Prince Alfred

The Connaught children, 1886. From left:
Prince Arthur, Princess Patricia, Princess
Margaret

Princess Alice of Albany, 1886

Prince Maurice of Battenberg, 1901

Prince Edward and Prince
Albert of York, 1897

Prince Edward of York, as portrayed on a ½
cent postage stamp, Newfoundland, 1897.
His first appearance on a stamp, this was one
denomination in a set which also featured
contemporary portraits of Queen Victoria,
the Prince and Princess of Wales, and the
Duke and Duchess of York

'The Royal Family 1897,
Four Generations', from
a printed cotton flag

The Prince of Wales and his brothers with Mr Hansell on their way to Crathie Church, c. 1907

'Royalty shopping'; Prince George and Prince John, 1907

Princess Elizabeth of Hesse and her Battenberg cousins in the children's playhouse at Schloss Wolfsgarten, Hesse, 1903. From left: Princess Louise of Battenberg, Prince Louis Francis of Battenberg, Princess Elizabeth, Prince George of Battenberg

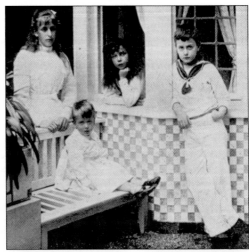

H.R.H. PRINCE EDWARD OF WALES. | H.R.H. PRINCE ALBERT OF WALES. | H.R.H. PRINCESS MARY OF WALES.

H.R.H. PR. HENRY OF WALES. | H.R.H. PR. GEORGE OF WALES. | H.R.H. PR. JOHN OF WALES.

The children of the Prince and Princess of Wales, from a series of Wills' cigarette cards, 1908. The complete set of 100 portrayed individual members of British and related European royalty

6

'A real atmosphere of love and happiness'

Princess Helena possessed no remarkable qualities. Plain and homely in appearance, uncomplicated in character, she became a stabilizing influence in the gloomy family circle where, at times, Queen Victoria hardly allowed her children to show any signs of cheerfulness lest they be misinterpreted as disrespect to their late father. Patient, with a no-nonsense attitude to life and quiet sense of efficiency, she became her mother's prop, and a useful secretary. If she was to get any freedom at all from her mother's beck and call, she realized, it would have to be in marriage. In 1865 she was introduced to Prince Christian of Schleswig-Holstein. Like her, he was no catch. Penniless by royal standards and balding, he appeared much older than his thirty-four years. Nevertheless, he was kindly, easy-going, a close friend of the Crown Prince and Princess of Prussia, and above all he harboured no objections to making his home in England near his mother-in-law as she considered her daughter much too useful to lose.

Helena and Christian were married on 5 July 1866, six weeks after her twentieth birthday. She was the first of the Queen's daughters to be granted the freedom of a honeymoon abroad, and they visited Paris, Interlaken and Genoa. On their return they moved into Frogmore House, and on 14 April 1867 she gave birth to her first son, named Christian Victor, at Windsor Castle. He was followed by a brother, Albert, in 1869, and two sisters, Helena Victoria in 1870 and two years later, shortly after a move to Cumberland Lodge in Windsor Great Park, Marie Louise. A third son, Harold, was born in 1874 but only lived for eight days, and a stillborn child followed the next year.

Despite these tragedies, Prince and Princess Christian's marriage was one of the most successful among Queen Victoria's children. The unambitious, unpretentious partners might have been made for each other. Unlike the Crown Prince and Princess of Prussia, they were not doomed to wait years for a throne until it was too late to reap the benefit; unlike the Prince and Princess of Wales, there was no incompatibility between their characters which made the marriage little more than one in name; and they never knew the unhappiness which would result in virtual separation between the as yet unmarried Prince Alfred and Princess Louise and their spouses.

The children enjoyed a relatively simple upbringing, notwithstanding the fact that their grandmother was their Queen. As Prince Christian was in effect unemployed, he had plenty of time to supervise their upbringing. He had always been devoted to children and he made an excellent father, teaching them German and giving them nightly lessons through the medium of German fairy tales. From their father, it was said, they learned 'the three lessons of the Persian boy of old, to ride, to shoot straight, and to tell the truth'. Others were sometimes called upon to assist in the educational process. 'I am so much obliged to you for telling me about that Nursery Governess,' the Princess wrote to Lady Bridport (7 January 1873), 'and I am sure had I wanted one, she might have suited – I think our boy too young yet to require a governess in the house – we have someone in to teach him for an hour in the day.'[1]

Healthy outdoor children, they learned to shoot at an early age. They were devoted to dogs and had two dachshunds, named Waldmann and Waldine. 'Other early amusements of ours,' recalled their son Albert, 'were hockey and cutting down trees in the park, in which we were much interested and constantly took part.'[2]

They played with the children of the household and of workers on the estate. They were taught cricket when they were about six by one of their father's footmen, and played with the sons of Colonel Gordon, their father's comptroller. Other early playfellows were Arthur Wellesley, son of the Dean of Windsor, and Edward Murdoch, son of Mr Charles Townshend Murdoch of Buckhurst, Wokingham, a veteran of the Rifle Brigade in the Crimea, and later MP for Reading. As they grew older, they took cricket and other organized games more and more seriously, bringing in a number of boys who were employed, or children of those employed, about the Great Park.

Prince and Princess Christian were very literary-minded. He loved poetry, and she had already translated her father's papers for an official memoir. For their sons' first tutor, in 1876, they engaged the poet F.W. Bourdillon, who commented on the boys' intelligence and on the depth of family affection he saw at Cumberland Lodge.

Though their daughters had their own personal maids, they were taught to dress themselves, fold their own clothes and tidy their own rooms. They dressed very simply; in winter they wore straight, blue-serge dresses and over these, in the schoolroom, Holland aprons bound with red or blue were worn. In the evening they had to change into left-over summer frocks, with high bronze-coloured kid boots buttoned up almost to their knees, and they always wore gloves out of doors. The latter were a source of some resentment, and in old age Princess Marie Louise thoroughly disliked having to wear gloves. Every summer they were put into plain white dresses, usually embroidered with broderie anglaise, and worn with a sash. The changeover invariably took place on 1 May, regardless of the temperature.

The Princesses were taught by French and German governesses, in order to improve their familiarity with both languages. When they were older a Frenchwoman, Madame de Goncourt, came twice a week to discuss French literature and European contemporary history with them, in French.

They also attended dancing classes in the Albert Institute at Windsor on Wednesday afternoons, where they were taught to dance and to have physical drill, considered so vital for their health and deportment. Prince Christian laid great stress on this aspect of his daughters' upbringing. They had to learn how to stand, rise, sit down gracefully, walk, above all how to curtsey and greet people and crowds with a little wave of the hand, a smile, and that vital slight inclination of the head.

Music played an important part in the Christians' family life. As an adult, Helena had outgrown the heavy-handedness on the piano which Miss Anderson had taken such pains to correct when she was smaller, and her musical friends included the singers Jenny Lind and Dame Clara Butt. The children were introduced to music and singing at an early age, and with his love of playing the piano it was evident that Christian Victor had inherited his mother's musical ear.

As part of their service to others, the children were encouraged to take an interest in medical and welfare work. Princess Christian was one of the original members of the Red Cross in Britain, and she was instrumental in initiating the State Registration of Nurses. Her sons and daughters took a close interest in medical work for the army, and even the young Marie Louise played her part with the others in 1877–8, rolling bandages to be sent out to the sick and wounded in the Russo-Turkish War.

The horrors of war rarely impinged on the consciousness of Queen Victoria's grandchildren in England, but for their cousins in Prussia, during the decade of Bismarck's conflicts, it was a different matter. Vicky dreaded the influence of Prussian militarism on her children, especially on her eldest son William, who showed evident signs of growing up in the old-fashioned Teutonic mould. She relished the chance to bring her children over to stay in Britain whenever possible.

Prince William's handicapped left arm was a severe trial, the effects of which were compounded by thoughtless treatment from so-called specialists. As a boy he was made to lift heavy weights with fingers that could barely grip an object at all, subjected to electric shocks mistakenly supposed to bring life to dead or imperfectly formed muscles, and strapped into a cage for an hour a day to correct the sideways tilt of his head caused by the different weight of his arms. None of these methods had any positive effect; on the contrary, they terrifed the young patient. Vicky and Fritz only allowed him to be subjected to them as they felt it held a chance, no matter how slender, of success.

What the boy really needed was to be surrounded by people who would accept his deformity and try to make light of it – as the Prince Consort would have doubtless done, had he lived long enough. The first stage occurred almost by accident, when as a boy of seven he was staying at Balmoral. One afternoon he wandered into the ghillies' room, where the men were cleaning the guns. He attempted to pick up a gun, but found it too heavy to lift with his good hand. Most of the men roared with laughter at his clumsiness, and he was about to scream with fury when one of them took the small rifle that had been the first gun of the Prince of Wales, put it in the boy's hand, and began to show him how to use it. From that day, William was taught that his bad arm need not be the insuperable barrier that everyone had supposed.

Queen Victoria always had a special place in her heart for this eldest grandchild. One of his fondest childhood memories was of an incident when he was twelve years old, and staying with her at Osborne House. One day Admiral Foley, a senior officer at Portsmouth, was invited to luncheon. A sailing frigate had recently been salvaged and towed into harbour, and the Queen wanted to know all the details. After they had exhausted this rather gloomy subject, she asked him how his sister was. Being rather deaf, he did not realize that the subject of conversation had changed. Still obsessed with the ship, he replied emphatically that he was going to have her turned over, take a good look at her bottom and have it well scraped. The Queen put down her knife and fork, and went into fits of hysterical laughter that soon had the rest of the family at table equally convulsed with mirth. The servants who were handing round dishes put them down and promptly hid behind the screen round the serving table, while the elderly admiral looked bewildered, wondering what all the amusement was about.

'Prussian pride' was a sin that had to be checked, but sometimes the Prussian children imbibed the wrong lessons from their mother. Princess Charlotte, on a visit to Balmoral in September 1871, haughtily refused to shake hands with John Brown, on the grounds that 'Mama says I ought not to be too familiar with servants'.[3] Whether the girl had been told not to be 'too familiar with servants' in general or not may be doubted. Yet Vicky, in common with most of her brothers and sisters, had no time for Brown, whose rude manners towards everybody were threatening to make the Queen, nicknamed behind her back 'the Empress Brown', a figure of ridicule.

Vicky never enjoyed the same rapport with her elder children as she did with the younger ones, all born after she had been able to assert herself and have more of a say in their upbringing. The younger ones (excluding her third son Sigismund, who died of meningitis at the age of twenty-one months) all enjoyed their English holidays with 'Grandmama' at her homes almost as much as their mother. Her youngest son Waldemar ('Waldie') was a particular favourite, and Vicky had high hopes for him. Of all the Queen's grandchildren, he was the one most interested in hunting for minerals and fossils on the Isle of Wight. He made a fine collection including fragments of fossilized coniferous wood, ammonite, and an iguanodon's tooth, all carefully labelled and deposited by his mother in the Swiss Cottage Museum.

By this time the museum had long since outgrown its modest accommodation in the cottage, and an adjacent building was erected in 1862 to house the ever-growing collections.* Beside Waldie's minerals could (and still can to this day) be seen foreign antiquities collected or preserved during royal tours, oriental *objets d'art*, statuettes, as well as minerals and archaeological specimens, granite from Balmoral, porphyry from Cornwall, fluorspar and quartz brought back from Weardale and parts of Durham by Affie in 1857, granite, vitreous sponges, shells, sharks' teeth and stalactites he found in Malta and Bermuda a few years later, and malachite, lapis lazuli, amethyst and jasper collected by him, Bertie and Arthur as boys. One of the most poignant displays in the museum is of Bulgarian children's costumes as worn by Johens and Georgy, two small boys rescued by Captain Hyde Parker of the Royal Navy at Kustendjeh while fleeing from the Turks in 1854. Brought back to safety in England, they were taken care of and educated by Queen Victoria, and they subsequently joined the Navy.

Affie's two eldest daughters, Marie and Victoria Melita, were particularly captivated by the fan shells, all tantalizingly beyond reach behind locked glass doors, safe from their busy fingers. Sometimes the custodian would unlock the door, and for a brief moment they would be allowed to hold one of the prize exhibits, a shell which was 'mysterious dark red but marked like tortoise - shell and of all marvels, it was double and had little spikes all over it.' To Marie, it was 'pure bliss' to be allowed to touch such a precious object.[4]

Waldie was devoted to animals and pets, on one occasion with unforeseen results. On a visit to Buckingham Palace, he arrived with a baby crocodile called Bob, which he let loose in the Queen's

*The museum collection was regularly added to until around 1900. In 1916 it was rearranged and amalgamated with certain items from the Swiss Cottage by Guy Laking, Keeper of the King's Armoury and Curator of the London Museum, who gave each object its own distinctive gold label.

room one day while she was busy at her papers. Her reaction at such an unexpected sight can readily be imagined, and her shrieks brought servants rushing in. None of them dared to pick Bob up, and Waldie had his share of helpless laughter at their expense before he agreed to put Bob back in his box.

He also showed a most un-Prussian devotion to cats and dogs, and after his death from diphtheria at the age of eleven, a loss from which his mother never really recovered, his favourite tabby cat showed a particular affection towards her. Sadly this did not save the animal from a brutal end. One morning a Prussian *jäger* saw her sitting in the garden, shot her, hung her body against a tree and cut off her nose. Her younger daughters, as bitterly distressed as she was, found some solace in burying the body in the garden beside a favourite dachshund. William, who evidently dismissed such love for pets as a ridiculous English sentiment, showed her no sympathy, thinking the *jäger* was showing laudable zeal as cats might harm pheasants. Queen Victoria was horrified: 'how distressed I am about your cat! it is monstrous – and the man ought to be hung on the tree'.[5]

Queen Victoria was passionate in her condemnation of cruelty to animals, though she was a lover of dogs rather than cats. Canines were more favoured by the British royal family, although Beatrice regularly had a cat. The feline appears less frequently in family photographs than dogs, one must assume, because of the difficulty in persuading one to remain still (unless asleep) long enough for the exposure needed by a camera in the nineteenth century. A theory that the Queen and her young children could not have cats because of the risk to Leopold being scratched by one does not hold water; cat scratches could easily be bound, and unlike internal bleeding or bruising, caused no serious risk to haemophiliacs. That the most tragic sufferer from the 'bleeding disease', the Queen's great-grandson Grand Duke Alexis, Tsarevich of Russia, adored (and was allowed to have) cats speaks for itself.

In the autumn of 1876 the Prince of Wales decided it was time to consider the next stage of his sons' education. Even their indulgent mother was becoming concerned at their perpetual quarrelling, 'using strong language to each other', presumably picked up in the stables, their tiresome inquisitiveness, regularly interrupting adults in their conversation, and playing havoc with games of croquet. The solution was for the boys to leave home. At length he made up his mind to send them both to the training ship *Britannia* for two years, leaving George with the option of choosing the Royal Navy as a career.

Mr Dalton felt that neither of the Princes, in his judgement, had reached the educational standard of the average private schoolboy of their age. Queen Victoria wanted Eddy to attend Wellington College. Dalton's misgivings were based on the inadvisability of separating the boys, as he wrote in a memorandum dated 11 February 1877:

> Prince Albert Victor requires the stimulus of Prince George's company to induce him to work at all. . . . The mutual influence of their characters on one another (totally different as they are in many ways) is very beneficial. . . . Difficult as the education of Prince Albert Victor is now, it would be doubly or trebly so if Prince George were to leave him. Prince George's lively presence is his mainstay and chief incentive to exertion; and to Prince George again, the presence of his elder brother is most wholesome as a check against that tendency to self-conceit which is apt at times to show itself in him. Away from his brother, there would be a great risk of his being made too much of and treated as a general favourite.[6]

Both Princes, he urged, should be entered as naval cadets on board *Britannia* at Dartmouth. The Queen objected, on the grounds that the very rough sort of life to which boys were exposed on board ship was not calculated 'to make a refined and amiable Prince, who in after years (if God spares him) is to ascend the throne. It would give him a very one-sided view of life which is not desirable.'[7]

Despite these objections, the Prince of Wales persuaded his mother to approve of both his sons going to sea as 'an experiment'. She assented, on condition that Dalton would continue to supervise them, and in September 1877 they joined the ship. They had their own cabin, but otherwise they were treated just as their fellow two hundred-odd cadets.

As expected, George made friends more easily with the other

cadets than the more reserved, diffident Eddy. He also took more of the knocks; the other boys made a point of 'taking it out' on them on the grounds that it would be their only chance. There was an unwritten rule than any cadet challenged by another to fight had to accept, and as Eddy was small for his age he was often made to challenge the larger ones. After coming off second best on several occasions, he suffered a heavy blow on the nose which made it bleed profusely. As a result the doctor forbade him to fight again.

The boys could buy sweets at the tuck shop at Dartmouth, as long as none were brought back on board ship. The bigger ones regularly asked George to bring them back something, but in this respect as in other things, he was allowed no privileges. All cadets were searched on returning to ship, and he was always punished if caught out as well as having his sweets confiscated. One shilling a week pocket money never went far enough, especially as the other cadets readily assumed that where royalty was involved there was plenty more where that came from, and never dreamed of paying him back.

Nevertheless, Prince George, or 'Sprat', a nickname derived from the diminutive of W(h)ales, made excellent progress in mathematics, and showed particular promise in the practical aspects of sailing and handling of boats. Dalton's first report to Queen Victoria from on board *Britannia* (14 November 1877), reassured her that the boys were in good health and very happy. Prince Albert Victor, he added with restraint, was not pulling his weight; there was no danger of 'the elder Prince working too hard, or overtaxing his powers, as Your Majesty seems to fear; in fact he might work harder than he does without any risk of detriment'.[8]

Holidays were spent at Sandringham, with occasional visits to Osborne and Abergeldie. At Osborne Prince George began to keep a diary, the first entry being made on 30 July 1878, recording a game of croquet with his Aunt Beatrice and then watching a cricket match between members of the household and the royal yacht. The diary ended on 12 August, a fortnight later, but he began a new one on 3 May 1880, which he continued until three days before his death fifty-five years later.

In the meantime, another royal family was growing up at Clarence House. In January 1874 Prince Alfred, created Duke of

Edinburgh in 1866, had married Grand Duchess Marie, only surviving daughter of Tsar Alexander II of Russia. Their only son, named Alfred after his father, was born on 15 October that year, followed by five daughters: Marie (1875), Victoria Melita (1876), Alexandra (1878), and after a stillborn daughter in 1881, Beatrice (1884). Clarence House was their London home, but in their affections it came a poor second to their country *pied-à-terre*, Eastwell Park, near Ashford in Kent. Like their grandmother, the young Edinburghs disliked London, 'and each time it was a grief when the season came for leaving Eastwell and the joys of the country for Clarence House, for smuts and smoke and gloomy walks in the Green Park'.[9]

Eastwell was full of delights for the children, inside and out. To them the vast house was a positive treasure-trove of unexplored rooms and passages. The back staircase was declared out-of-bounds to them by the governess, who said it was 'no place for little girls', probably as she feared they would fall through the railings. Thus was a challenge issued to them to go exploring; peeping through the rails made them feel giddy, but 'something stronger than fear' impelled them to persevere. Halfway down the stairs was a mysterious corner which the servants called the 'Glory Hole', another place 'not for little girls'. They never succeeded in exploring it, though they imagined it was probably a private pantry. Whenever they were seen looking down the banisters, they were quickly sent back upstairs.

Outside, few other attractions could compare with a vast tree, which had such a large hole that young Alfred and his three eldest sisters could all sit in it at once. It was the centre of their outdoor games for a long time, where they could play at being Robinson Crusoe, Robin Hood and his merry men, Red Indians, pirates, or whatever else took their fancy. In the middle of this sylvan retreat was an intrusive branch which they decided would have to be removed with a saw or an axe. They begged their father to let them have the tools, but he would only allow them a saw. 'An axe would take off a finger at one blow,' he pointed out, 'whilst you would soon enough stop sawing if you began sawing your finger!'[10]

Their mother played a greater part in their lives than their father, recalled Marie ('Missy') in her memoirs: 'he, being a sailor, was often away from home; he was even a little bit of a stranger to us'.[11] Basically a shy man, the Duke was more at ease with his contemporaries and the role of playful father did not come easily to him. He had a habit of looking through the children sometimes as if they were not there. This was a curious characteristic of all Queen Victoria's children as adults at one time or other, and the Edinburghs found their uncles and aunts oddly absent-minded. They would occasionally become aware of a youngster in their presence, start a conversation with him or her and then wander off, leaving the child feeling rather hurt and dismayed.

Nevertheless, Affie loved to join in with his children's games. A particular favourite, kept for long winter evenings, involved putting the lamps out, while he would hide in a dark corner pretending to be an ogre. They had no idea which room he was in as, trembling with excitement, they crawled through the darkness. When they were on the point of giving up, he would catch them off their guard and spring out, his growls and their hysterical shrieks and laughter ringing through the passages. To Marie, 'it was a gruesome game and gave us the real thrill that danger gives to adventurers'.[12]

Snow was rare at Eastwell, but one winter it fell thickly, and he took the children out tobogganing down a hill near the dairy. Skating was another winter activity they enjoyed eagerly, father and youngsters wearing their best black velvet caps trimmed with Russian sable, as much a part of the skating expeditions as the hot cinnamon-flavoured red wine with which they refreshed themselves afterwards.

At Christmas a tree was set up in the big library, while presents were laid out on white-covered tables all round the walls of the room. Affie became as eager as a child himself, planning everything meticulously, and could get very angry if the smallest detail was overlooked. The children found it particularly thrilling to stir the servants' plum pudding. It took place in the stewards' room, and in the official part of the stables, as 'house and stables were two separate realms and one never dared overlap the other'. An enormous bowl was set upon the table and each child had to take turns with the stirring. At last Christmas Eve came, and the library doors, which had been closed for several days, were thrown open. There stood the tree, a blaze of light, and all around upon the white-decked tables, one mass of gifts for everybody, nobody ever being forgotten. The children stepped forward, holding hands, spellbound at the scene as presents were distributed in a blaze of candlelight, 'accompanied by that delicious fragrance of singed fir-branches so inseparable from Christmas'.[13]

Living at Green Park was not without its compensations. Outside, almost opposite the entrance to Buckingham Palace, stood a balloon man. It was a treat for the Edinburgh princesses when their governess produced a few pennies from her pocket and they were allowed to buy themselves a few balloons, or airballs as Marie sometimes called them. She found the smell 'irresistibly nasty, so that we were forever rubbing our noses against them.' They were not slow to discover the piercing noise – half squeak, half groan – that could be made when drawing their fingers across the taut surfaces of these brightly-coloured 'bubbles of enchantment'.[14]

As a mother, the Duchess of Edinburgh tempered kindness with severity. In an undemonstrative way, she adored her children and encouraged them in their carefree garden activities, letting them run around, skate, climb trees, and enjoy a healthy outdoor life. But she attached great importance to a strict upbringing. They must always be ready to talk and entertain people; nothing, she told them, was more hopeless or rude than a prince or princess who never opened his or her mouth. When invited out for meals, they must never insult their hosts by refusing what was put in front of them, or even leaving the slightest scrap. If the food made them feel sick, they would have to wait until they got home. Every food, she impressed on them, was digestible for a good stomach, but the English spoilt their digestion from earliest childhood by imagining that they could not eat 'this or that'. 'Digestions' were 'a most unpleasant subject and not drawing-room conversation.'

The Duchess enjoyed robust health, and never allowed her children to complain about minor ailments like colds or headaches. Fevers did not send them to bed. In this she resembled Queen Victoria, of whom it was said that the only excuse for not attending dinner was sudden death. Yet the smallest indisposition never went unnoticed, and she was always ready with discreetly administered pills or medicines. English doses, to her, were much stronger than Continental doses and she would call them *des remèdes de cheval*.

In 1882 the artist John Everett Millais was commissioned by the Queen to paint a portrait of Princess Marie of Edinburgh to be exhibited at the Royal Academy that summer. In the biography by his son, Millais 'thought it would be well to show the multitude that, though of high degree, the little Princess was by no means brought up to lead an idle and useless life, but was taught to work for others, if not for herself; so he designedly presented her holding her knitting in her hands.' The Duke of Edinburgh was guest of honour at a banquet in May given to mark the opening of the exhibition, and in his speech he paid special thanks to Millais 'for the admirable way in which he has perpetuated, and the charming manner in which he has drawn the features of my little girl'.[15]

In personal and political terms, the Edinburghs' marriage was not a success. It went against the grain for a senior officer in the British Navy to be married to a Russian Grand Duchess, at a time when Anglo-Russian tensions were never far below the surface. Memories of the Crimean War, during which Russian imperial pride had suffered a severe blow to her prestige after defeat by the combined British and French forces, were still within living memory of most people. Britain still distrusted Russian designs on the Balkans and Middle East, and war between Britain and Russia was only narrowly averted during the first four years of their marriage. The Duchess of Edinburgh made no secret of her dislike for her in-laws or her contempt for Britain, and despite a shared love of music, the Duke and Duchess had little in common. Perhaps it was as well for the children that their father's naval duties kept him away from home so much.

Young Alfred, as he was always known, was separated from the family at an early age to be educated in Coburg, where it was assumed he would succeed his father as Duke. The girls had their lessons at home, in England, later in Malta (when the Duke was stationed there as Commander-in-Chief of the Mediterranean Fleet) and finally in Coburg. Alfred had the misfortune to be placed under the care of a tyrannical tutor, cryptically named 'Dr X' in Marie's memoirs. An arrogant, tyrannical German, he hated everything English, and did his best to uproot the young Edinburghs' Anglophile affections. He could be an excellent companion, tell stories well, and talk with authority on any subject from history, geography and botany, to art and social questions. But he was impatient, intolerant, and could never resist ridiculing Prince Alfred before others. His bullying behaviour was calculated to destroy any self-confidence the boy might have had, and his sisters fiercely resented this callous treatment.

When they followed him out to Coburg, they ran up not only against him but also their governess, 'Fraülein', who later became betrothed and married to Dr X. They were two of a kind; she was outwardly charming and friendly, but determined to do as much harm as she could. She persuaded the Duchess that it would be as well to counter any signs of vanity in the girls by forcing them to wear ugly clothes, harsh linen, coarse calico, badly-shaped shoes, and ugly gowns, hats and cloaks. She would encourage them to ask her about 'the hidden mysteries of life', and then show them up to their mother as 'nasty little girls with unhealthy minds'.

In the rebellious Victoria Melita, or 'Ducky', they met their match one day. A large silver cup, filled with flowers or a plant, always stood in the centre of the dining table. When the Duchess was away Fraülein sat at the head, Dr X at the foot. This cup prevented the adoring couple from gazing fondly into each other's eyes at meals. After putting up with this obstacle for some time, Dr X high-handedly ordered a servant to take it away. The girls immediately protested; Mama had put it there, she alone had the right to order its removal, and as they were her children they could not allow it to be touched. Dr X tried to laugh away their objections, but finding they would not give way, he exclaimed with contempt, 'Well, it is either I or the pot!' Ducky stretched out her arms, clasped the cup to her chest, and glared at him. 'We prefer the pot!' she shouted. With as much dignity as he could muster, the defeated tutor left the table, and the rest of the meal was passed in silence.

Not all those placed in authority above them were so hateful. A particular favourite was Miss Butler, their music mistress. None of the girls had inherited their parents' musical talent and her efforts to teach them the piano were marked with limited success, but she became and remained a firm friend until after they were married with their own families. Miss Butler was too indulgent and too fond of them 'to be an efficient instructor to a trio of unruly children not overblessed with musical aptitude'.

At Coburg the girls had several tutors who attempted to teach them different subjects with varying degrees of success. The Princesses evidently shared their grandmother's aversion to the finer (or not so fine) points of human and animal biology. This was rather a disadvantage to Dr Heim, who taught them natural history and botany. 'We had an instinctive horror of anything describing inner organs, we thought it had an air of butchery about it that was not quite decent,' Missy recalled, 'and we were nearly sick when one day, full of enthusiasm, he brought us an ox's eye so as to demonstrate the marvels of the optic organzation. No, decidedly we were not of the modern school which unblushingly inquires into every detail of the human mechanism.'[16]

The Duchess of Edinburgh spoke perfect English, but reluctantly. She preferred French, saying that it was by far the most elegant language and that a beautiful letter could only be written in French. Most of her daughters' early thank-you letters to Queen Victoria for birthday and Christmas presents were in French. It was typical of the Duchess's hard-to-satisfy nature that she did not like France as a nation. Her daughters hated speaking French, which they they thought 'an affected language, a language for grown-ups, not for children, and we wilfully threw away all the good opportunities of absorbing the language properly'.[17]

Prince Alfred of Edinburgh was always delicate, but his sisters were lively, attractive and healthy. They compared favourably with their Wales cousins, unkindly if not inaccurately dubbed 'their royal shynesses'. Apart from Maud, the Wales Princesses had little of their mother's beauty or zest for life. They were regarded as a mutual admiration society in their own exclusive world at Sandringham. They believed that they had been poured directly from the salt cellar of God. To their closest friends, Louise was 'Toots', Victoria 'Gawks' and Maud 'Snipey'. The family nickname for Maud was 'little Harry', after Admiral Harry Keppel, a friend of the Prince of Wales. They relished visits to their mother's parents in Copenhagen, where they were spoiled outrageously, but not the prospect of their sterner Grandmama at home. Once as they were getting ready with great reluctance to leave Sandringham for Balmoral, Louise and Victoria were in floods of tears, while the less easily intimidated Maud stamped her foot and declared, 'I won't go!'

The Princess of Wales was ill at ease in her husband's circle. Though they were more compatible as personalities than the Duke and Duchess of Edinburgh, the future King Edward VII's infidelities, his boredom at home, and his wife's deafness, rheumatism, and subsequent disenchantment with society life drove a wedge between them. As a result she turned more towards her children and animals for companionship. Her sons having left, or 'escaped' to a life on the ocean wave, she dominated her daughters. Before leaving home, Prince George had always read to her during the ritual of hair-brushing, and every evening he would say his prayers with her like a little child. From her he learnt the simple direct religious faith and practice that characterized him throughout life, daily Bible-reading, regular attendance at church and at Communion. Her letters to him were artless, full of expressions as 'What a bad old Motherdear not to write and you were quite right to say "naughty, naughty!"'[18] Such letters could never have been written by Queen Victoria to her sons.

The Princess did not encourage her children to grow up. Even when he was nineteen, she wrote to Prince George, hoping to find him 'the same and unchanged in every respect', which he appeared to regard as entirely natural. Louise wrote to their father's secretary, Francis Knollys, when he was in Ireland, that she was 'practising her steps for the tiresome court ball, that Gawks is going to bed instead like Cinderella, and that Snipey is trying to console herself with a song instead of singing her hymns in Church as she ought to do. . . . We are afraid you won't be at all glad to see us *country bumpkins* again, as we shall have nothing to talk about but cows and cowslips!'[19] Hardly the kind of letter to be expected from somebody of eighteen.

Other people's children could expect the same kindly but embarrassing prolonged childhood from the future Queen Alexandra. Some years later, when she was Queen, she sent her niece Princess Patricia of Connaught presents suitable for a girl of ten, in a parcel delivered by a footman (well-conditioned by years of royal service to keep a straight face in situations bordering on the farcical) with the verbal message, 'To darling little Patsy from her silly old Aunt Alix'. 'Darling little Patsy' was in her early twenties and almost six foot tall.[20]

The Wales Princesses were born collectors. They loved to show others their vast accumulations of neatly arranged animals in bronze, china, and stone, rows of miniature vases, tiny photograph frames, watercolours of gardens and 'sweet-faced ladies'. There were pictures of daffodils, of Windsor Castle in a mist, portraits of favourites horses, dogs and friends, and photographs in which the face of 'Motherdear' was ever dominant.

In 1879 Prince Christian Victor of Schleswig-Holstein became a boarder at school at Bracknell. The following year he passed his entrance examination for Wellington College. As the Prince and Princess of Wales had rejected the Queen's suggestion that their sons should go to the school in the founding of which the Prince Consort had taken such an interest, she was gratified that at least one of her grandsons would be enrolled there.

Christian Victor was the first member of the royal family to attend public school. Entering the college on 25 January 1881, it was made clear from the start that he was to be treated as an ordinary boy, with no privileges. His housemaster, the Revd Charles William Penny, left an amusing record in his diary of the upheaval his illustrious pupil's arrival inadvertently caused that day:

HRH Prince Christian arrived suddenly at 2.30: front hall full of the —'s luggage; drawing-room full of —s and —'s tutor. Hustled them out. All my nice little plans disarranged for a formal reception with Mellon (the manservant) full dressed. As soon as I could I hustled the —s into my study, and was as polite as I could be to the Prince; we went upstairs and saw the valet unpack his clothes and put them into his drawers. Fortunately Speer (the carpenter) was in the house, and I got him at once to hang up the pictures and put up the Prince's own bookcase in place of the one I had put up for him. Then we went and saw Wickham, and then we returned and I gave them tea in the drawing-room. Then the Prince went upstairs and was alone with his son for a little while. At a quarter to four Prince Christian departed and I promised to write on Sundays to say how the boy was getting on. I particularly asked if I should write to him or to Colonel Gordon, and he said to himself.[21]

Predictably, the schoolmasters were effusive about the progress of their new pupil. A few weeks later, Prince Christian asked for a report about his son, and they wrote back glowingly that he had 'made a most favourable impression upon us all by his simple, unaffected demeanour and his desire to identify himself with the life of his school-fellows'.[22]

On 26 February he was granted his first exeat. Mr Penny took him to Wokingham to see him off in the train to join his family at Cumberland Lodge.

At the end of his first term the report mentioned that he was good at divinity, fair in Latin, much better in German (his father had evidently prepared the ground thoroughly), and poor in French, with 'defective knowledge of grammar due to want of concentrated attention during lessons'. Taking advantage of the chance to expand his musical education, he took violin and organ lessons. After giving some thought to a future career, which he considered lay in the army, his parents and masters decided that he should study for Woolwich or Sandhurst, and give up Latin in favour of science.

In March 1882, after an epidemic of measles (which he escaped) at school, the three-week holiday at Easter was extended, as the whole College had to be disinfected and whitewashed, and the sanatorium needed to be free of boys for a full fortnight before school could reopen.

At Wellington, it was considered, he first began to find his royal status somewhat irksome. Teachers had noted from the start that he was anxious to be 'one of the crowd' and identify himself in every way with his schoolfellows. One evening he was watching the professional coaching of the school cricket XI, one of whom allowed him to go in and bat. After ten minutes at the crease the professional, not recognizing his small pupil, judged him 'a most promising youngster'. Cricket soon became an abiding passion. It had always been a favourite game from childhood, and friends believed he enjoyed it particularly because it depended on skill alone.

In other spheres, he found that being royal was a hindrance. Any success he achieved would be attributed to his rank; yet because of this rank, those in authority above him were always keen to protect him, denying him freedom of action. Cricket was different, a great leveller, and by the time he began his third year at Wellington, the game was taking up so much of his time that his father complained he was too keen on getting into the XI that he was neglecting his academic studies, becoming careless at spelling, and not reading enough books for amusement: 'it is my constant complaint during the holidays that I never see him read a book'.[23] The masters tactfully but firmly defended him, pointing out that he was working very hard, and indeed he achieved his ambition of getting into the XI.

From a series of letters to 'Raphael', presumably a friend who had recently left, cricket was the first love of his schooldays.

> You must think me a brute for not having written before but cricket has taken up all my time, Midge has got his 2nd XI [the Prince wrote towards the end of the summer term, 20 July 1884]. I get horribly humbuged about it because I am always waking with him & going up to the house on Sundays. But I don't give a d— what the fellows say. Every one in the XI voted when we made up the 2nd XI . . . Please excuse the Coll[ege] paper & the writing but I am writing this in the Algebra Exam, & as you know I always had a more intimate acquaintance with 'square leg' than 'square root'. Also the curve I am most acquainted with is that 'peculiar' one which is often followed by a fall of the stumps. Excuse these bad puns but I am awfully on the spot . . . You must come over one of these days & see us here we are having the deuce of a spree here this term, & I am half fused today for I was drinking claret cup with the Midge yesterday & after that Toze collared me up & he is simply mad about it.[24]

He passed his preliminary examination for Sandhurst in 1884, and left Wellington at Christmas the following year. Mr Penny's final reports of him were glowing. In his half-term report, he wrote, he had 'never had a Prefect who more earnestly tried to help me or who more regularly and considerately discharged his various duties,'[25] and at the end of term, he noted that the Prince had endeared himself to all the staff 'by his uniform sweetness of temper, his unfailing courtesy and unaffected modesty and simplicity of character. During the whole five years that he has been as it were a member of my family, we have never had the least trouble or anxiety. And to every member of our household the Prince has been a courteous gentleman.'[26]

Not all royal pupils behaved themselves so well at school. Prince

Francis of Teck, reputedly the cleverest and most amusing of the brothers of the future Queen Mary, was enrolled at Wellington a little later. His time there was cut short when he threw the headmaster over a hedge in order to win a bet, and was promptly expelled.

In May 1878 Arthur, now Duke of Connaught, became engaged to Princess Louise of Prussia. The months of preparation for the wedding were overshadowed by the death of his sister Alice, Grand Duchess of Hesse, from diphtheria, that December – ironically, on the seventeenth anniversary of the Prince Consort's death – but court mourning was suspended for the ceremony at Windsor on 13 March 1879. The Duke had never been a disappointment to the Queen, who could not speak highly enough of her son. At one point, she confided rather possessively to Vicky that Arthur was so good that he did not need to get married at all.

They set up house at Bagshot Park, Surrey, and on 15 January 1882 the couple's first daughter, named Margaret, was born. As she grew older she was known as 'Princess Daisy'. She was joined in the nursery on 13 January 1883 by a brother, Arthur, and another sister, Patricia, on 17 March 1886. The Duchess of Connaught passed on her artistic talents, and her love of animals, to the children. Margaret became a gifted painter, and all of them enjoyed being taken to the stables to help their mother feed the horses with sugar. When a model dairy under the Duchess's directions was built at Bagshot, helping to make butter and cheese was a hobby eagerly shared by them all.

Meanwhile Leopold, the 'child of anxiety' whom Queen Victoria had hardly dared to expect to reach maturity, was created Duke of Albany in April 1881, and in November that year became engaged to Princess Helen of Waldeck-Pyrmont, sister of Queen Emma of the Netherlands. They were married on 27 April 1882 at Windsor.

Their first child, a daughter named Alice, was born on 25 February 1883. When the Queen first set eyes on the baby, Leopold was recovering from a bad knee on one sofa, and Helen was resting on another. When the Queen, leaning heavily on her stick, hobbled in 'as a third helpless creature, it had quite a ludicrous effect'.

Sadly, Leopold died thirteen months later. On medical advice he was sent to Cannes to avoid the worst of the winter weather in March 1884. He slipped on a staircase at his hotel, and died from a brain haemorrhage. Helen was expecting a second child, and the posthumous son and heir, Charles ('Charlie'), was born at Claremont on 19 July 1884. Sir William Harcourt was the cabinet minister appointed to certify the birth, and before his departure from Claremont next day he left a letter to the Duchess, offering his heartfelt congratulations on the happy event: 'God has granted you a son of consolation in your great sorrow and I pray that the little child I was so happy to welcome into this world may grow up to be a comfort and support to you.'[27]

The other royal grandchildren were obliged to take their part in court mourning. From Cumberland Lodge, Christian Victor wrote to Raphael (26 April), apologizing for the long gap in correspondence, 'only as you know my uncle died suddenly & there was such loads of things to do & I really have had scarcely any time to myself. My holidays were not very brilliant at first but since my grandmother has been at Darmstadt I have been allowed to play cricket & shoot rabbits, which I might not do as long as she was here.'[28]

Princess Alice of Albany, who lived to a record age for any member of the British royal family – ninety-seven years and ten months – long retained vivid memories of her fatherless childhood at Claremont with her mother and brother Charlie. There was mother in deepest black for a long time after her husband's death, before she changed into a pale grey summer dress; 'Nanna Creak' who found that 'delicate, nervous and tiresome baby brother' got on her nerves so much that she had to go; and there were expeditions to feed wild ducks on the lake at Claremont with baskets of dry bread cut into squares, though Alice enjoyed eating the bread herself.

Their household included Frederick, the nursery footman, 'rather a rough diamond' with a drink problem, who brought their meals up from down in the basement, and Mr Long, the butler, who carried the children upstairs. Every day they demanded him to explain the story behind a print, '*La Dernière Cartouche*', of the Franco-Prussian War. There was an under-butler, Benton, whose family they visited regularly, various footmen, housemaids, housekeepers and a nursemaid who married the footman, Jo, a lovable yet curious-looking individual with curly black hair and a wall-eye. There was also Mrs Lawley, with a lace cap and little twisted curls at each side, who gave the children sugar candy on long strings from her store cupboard. She served the family faithfully until she was eighty, and on her birthday the Duchess of Albany had a large birthday cake made, bearing eighty small candles. All these people played an important part in their young lives, 'and so we grew up in a real atmosphere of love and happiness, but with scarcely any outside contacts'.[29]

Only at Windsor did they mix with their young relations. The Queen would regularly invite her daughter-in-law and grandchildren, and they always came by train. To young Alice, there was 'something indescribable' about the castle, or the 'Sovereign's Entrance', as she called it – a special Windsor Castle smell, 'a smell like nowhere else – old furniture kept very clean, flowers and, altogether, a special delicious and welcoming smell that only now is fading away'.[30]

There was a unique aura to the whole place, from the page who escorted them in, the housekeeper in black silk and a lace cap at the door, and the equerry-in-waiting, to the wide corridor at the castle 'with all its treasures which one accepted yet never noticed'. Their nanny was always admonishing them to curtsy at the door, kiss their grandmother's hand, behave themselves and not make a noise in her presence, until they were quite filled with awe. Once they met her, she was less intimidating. She would sit writing at her table while they played with their toys and built walls with her despatch boxes. In the same room was a spinning wheel and a glass containing the water for twisting the wool, which they loved to play with – and were invariably scolded by her for doing so.

Alice's bedroom was on the ground floor at Claremont. When she was four, she was awakened one night by a burglar who had got into the room through the open window, with the aid of a ladder stolen from the nearby farmhouse, two accomplices following him. The incident was reported in several newspapers. One stated that it had occurred in January when the infant Princess had not yet got over the Christmas festivities and was overjoyed to think that Father Christmas had returned so soon. Others stated that she asked the burglar why he had come through the window instead of the chimney, why was he not wearing a white beard and red coat, and why were his associates so untraditionally attired. To the best of her memory, the incident occurred in the autumn, not after Christmas.

She refused to be taken in by her mother's soothing explanation that it was a visit from Father Christmas. Alice had heard the nurse's screams, which woke everyone and forced the burglars to beat a hasty retreat.

The young Alice was educated by a governess, Jane Potts, who came when Alice was seven and stayed for eleven years. 'We emerged from the nursery very stuffy little things,' Alice remembered. Miss Potts made them climb fences, pick up apples and took them for delightful long walks. She was responsible for firing them with a tremendous love of history, encouraging them to play at acting out Roman wars, assuming the names and characters of their favourite heroes. It was the same with Greek history, and Alice and Charlie used to quarrel over Darius and Alexander the Great, as Alice always chose the victor. She was Julius Caesar and Charlie was Pompey. A friend, Kitty, was Croesus, though she knew nothing about her role. They always acted people out of books they read. Though Alice feared that Miss Potts must have had a very dull and lonely time, she evidently realized how quiet their lives were at that time, and put up with all their games and sham fights during their walks in the Claremont woods.

Every evening before dinner, Alice knitted or did needlework while the Duchess of Albany read aloud to them. Starting off with Henty, Charlotte Yonge, and Molesworth, she introduced them to Dickens, Scott, Kingsley, and R.L. Stevenson when they were older. Knitting was not always the drudge for them that it might have been for other children. As a reward, and to tempt them to help her, one day the Duchess wrapped a collection of little bronze animals in paper and then wound them inside a great ball of wool for the children to find. They were enchanted with the animals, and kept them in tins given to them by Lewis Carroll with pictures from *Alice in Wonderland* on the sides, and their own names scratched by him on the bottom.

Lewis Carroll, or more correctly Dr Charles Lutwidge Dodgson, was particularly kind to Alice and Charlie. When Alice was five, she attended a party at Hatfield, and he was telling a story. He was afflicted with a stammer, and she had some difficulty following his story. She asked suddenly in a rather loud voice, 'Why does he waggle his mouth like that?' She was quickly removed by the lady-in-waiting. Afterwards he wrote that he 'liked Charlie but thought Alice would turn out badly'. Yet she was soon forgiven, and he gave them books for Christmas with anagrams of their names on the fly-leaf.

The Duchess continued to have a number of her husband's literary and artistic friends from Oxford to stay at Claremont. The children found they seemed very old, but they were always kind, and after tea the children invariably brought out an illustrated *Comic History of England* which they never tired of showing to the guests.

In winter Alice recalled being dressed in a thick frock, covered by a pinafore with lace at the neck and shoulders, long black stockings and button boots. Like her cousin Princess Marie Louise of Schleswig-Holstein, she changed into summer outfits of cotton frocks on 1 May, regardless of the temperature. The summers, she thought, like many an adult of advancing years reminiscing on the joys of childhood, 'seem to have lasted longer than nowadays'.

When Charlie grew out of, or as Alice put it, became 'too much for' Miss Potts, he became a day boarder at the nearby Sandroyd School, riding there daily on Puck, a Shetland pony. Later he went to prep school at Lyndhurst, while Alice stayed at home to be taught by Miss Potts. In due course she went to London for drawing classes and instruction in chemistry and literature, while Charlie entered Eton.

As Queen Victoria had 'lost' her other children, she decided that her youngest daughter – still 'Baby' – must always remain with her as confidante and secretary. However, in the summer of 1884 Beatrice had fallen in love with the dashing Prince Henry of Battenberg, whose elder brother Louis had recently married her niece, Princess Victoria of Hesse. The Queen was furious, and for several weeks mother and daughter communicated merely by means of written notes across the breakfast table. However, Beatrice had a will of her own as well – she was not her mother's daughter for nothing – and stood firm. The Queen was persuaded, particularly by Vicky, that 'Baby' should be allowed to marry her 'Liko'. At last she gave her consent, on condition that Prince Henry would retire from the Prussian army, and live with his wife and mother-in-law in England.

The young couple married on 23 July 1885 at St Mildred's Church, Whippingham, and their marriage gave Queen Victoria a new lease of life. Once more there was a man in the family, and moreover one who was not in awe of her. Henry could make light-hearted conversation with her and encourage her to laugh at meals. Christmas 1885 was the happiest at Osborne since the last time the Prince Consort had presided over the festivities. Beatrice and Liko were allocated a suite in the new wing, Helen of Albany and her children, the Duke and Duchess of Connaught and theirs, were there to share presents on the tables, party games, theatrical performances, and watch beech logs burning brightly in the polished steel grate of the Queen's sitting-room.

On 23 November 1886 at Windsor, Beatrice gave birth to a son. The baby inadvertently caused a change in royal routine. Christmas had always been spent at Osborne, but the Queen decided that it would be unwise to make the young mother and child travel so soon, and they stayed at the castle. Here he was christened on 18 December. Despite a suggestion from *Punch* that in view of the coming year's anniversary 'the Battenberg Baby should be called Prince JUBILEE', he was given the names Alexander Albert. The first was in honour of his uncle 'Sandro', the ill-fated sovereign Prince of Bulgaria, who had been forced by Russian agents to abdicate his throne a few weeks earlier, and had arrived in England a virtual exile. The christening was held in the White Drawing Room, where the gold font with figures of naked children playing round its base was used.

It seemed as if no grandchild had given the Queen more pleasure than the arrival of this thirty-seventh child.* The family noticed how cheerful she now became. According to legend, some days later a small boy ran beside her carriage at Windsor to get a better view of her. She ordered the coachman to stop, and handed her young admirer a florin. She did the same for a blind man singing 'Abide with me' by Windsor Bridge.

During a respite after the busy summer and the Golden Jubilee celebrations in London the following summer, the family moved north to Balmoral, where Beatrice produced a daughter on 24 October 1887. She was the first royal child to be born in Scotland since the future King Charles I had entered the world

---

*Thirty-ninth, if two who had been stillborn were included.

in 1600. The locals were delighted at the news, and even more so when told that the christening would be on Deeside. No royal child had been christened in Scotland since Prince Henry, son of King James VI, in 1594. The former Empress Eugenie of the French, who had been staying at Abergeldie earlier that season, was invited to be one of the sponsors, and the baby was baptized Victoria Eugenia Julia Ena – the last name in error, as the rector misread the handwritten documents which had specified her last name was to be 'Eua'.

On 21 May 1889 Beatrice had another son at Windsor, named Leopold in honour of the brother to whom she had been so close. Three days later the Queen celebrated her seventieth birthday, and the two elder Battenberg children went to her bedroom, 'Drino' shyly holding a nosegay as he wished 'Gangan' many happy returns.

Just over two years later, on 3 October 1891, a third son to Beatrice and Henry was born at Balmoral. His birth in Scotland was a signal for great celebrations. The gold font was brought up from the south, and a battery of artillery discharged the royal salute. A bonfire was built on the top of Craig Gowan, with a procession of pipers, followed by ghillies, cottars and keepers, carrying flaming pine torches, marching up the hill to light a blaze that could be seen for miles around Deeside. With whisky to fortify them on their way, they danced on the flat rocky space reserved for such occasions. At the end of October, the baby was christened in the drawing-room at Balmoral. The Queen held him proudly, dressed in the historic christening robe worn by so many princes and princesses before him, and by her side stood the father, wearing the Royal Stuart tartan. The names given to Queen Victoria's fortieth and last grandchild were Maurice Victor Donald, the last as a compliment to the people of Scotland.

The young Battenbergs were of the same generation as the young Connaughts and Albanys, and the three groups of cousins were regular playmates. Most of the other cousins were already grown up, but sometimes they were happy to join in their games, in particular giving the smaller children pick-a-back rides. It was a heart-rending occasion for the adults in November 1888 when Vicky, the once young and optimistic Princess Royal, returned for a visit to her homeland five months after the death from cancer of her beloved husband, Emperor Frederick III. With her came their three younger, unmarried daughters, all dressed in deepest mourning. 'Those cousins were lovely to us,' Alice of Albany recalled, 'and raced each other with Charlie and me seated pick-a-back on their bustles.'[31]

7

'I don't see the wings'

Much as she still disliked babies, in old age Queen Victoria enjoyed the company of young children, and seemed more tolerant towards adolescents. Age had mellowed her, and she became a kindly old lady. She found it much easier to get on with her grandchildren than her own children. It was good to have granddaughters staying with her, particularly the motherless son and daughters of Alice, in whom she took a special protective interest after the tragic weeks of winter 1878.

In November that year Princess Victoria had contracted diphtheria which spread rapidly to her brother, sisters and father. Only Elizabeth, the second daughter, escaped as she had gone to stay with relatives before the infection started. The youngest child, four-year-old May, succumbed, and Ernie was close to death at one stage. From Darmstadt, their lady-in-waiting, Wilhelmine de Grancy, took up the sad story, writing to Lady Fanny Howard (17 November):

> our dear, sweet Princess May has not been able to resist the dreadful illness. She died very suddenly in the night before last. The Grand Duke, Prince Ernie and the three Princesses are, thank God, getting better. Yesterday Prince Ernie was still *very* ill and seriously in danger. What an anxiety for the poor Grand Duchess, besides the bitter grief of losing that sweet child. May God help her, she must hide her sorrow before them, till they are better. I have not seen her. I have been absent for the last eight weeks and just as I was coming back I got a telegram to say I was not to do so; till yesterday I got another telling me to come, and I am here since this morning but not at the Palace . . . I long to see her, oh how much, but I must be patient, it is at least better to be here, near her; to be away was almost more than I could bear.[1]

The children recovered, but Alice caught the infection and in her weakened state she stood no chance. She died on 14 December, the anniversary of her father's death; in Queen Victoria's words, the coincidence was 'almost incredible and most mysterious'. Among her adult granddaughters none, perhaps, was closer to her than Princess Victoria of Hesse. As Alice's eldest child, she virtually took on the role of mother to the children when their father Grand Duke Louis was left a widower.

Queen Victoria, the Princess recalled with admiration and detachment many years later, was invariably gracious to her grandchildren, but still expected perfect manners and immediate obedience from them, and any offender would be left in no doubt as to her displeasure. 'These are the years of Angeli's portrait, with its stern and rather forbidding expression of face. My mother's death broke through many of these outward barriers and the constant signs of affectionate pity and interest, gave to our intercourse a more natural ease.'[2]

Though she had been strict with the elder grandchildren, the younger generation – particularly the young Connaughts and Battenbergs – found that she had mellowed with the proverbial grandmother's leniency by then. After the gloom of her early widowhood, when most signs of outward amusement had been severely frowned upon, the Queen's natural Hanoverian high spirits reawakened.

Like her children, contemporary relatives and close friends, all her grandchildren would receive special personal letters on their birthdays with presents, usually toys for the boys, or jewellery for the girls. 'I hope you like the pearls & *watch?*' the Queen wrote to Princess Victoria of Hesse (5 April 1874), wishing her a happy eleventh birthday. 'It belonged to me as a child – & as it has a V on it – I thought it would do for you.'[3] The grandchildren often responded with items of carefully crafted handiwork as presents. In May 1888 the Edinburgh Princesses, then living at San Antonio Palace on Malta, made her a quilt which the Duke and Duchess brought to England on a brief visit at around the time of her birthday.

Despite the ageing Queen's indulgence, there were limits as to what the youngsters could get away with. The eldest child of Princess Victoria of Hesse, by then Princess Louis of Battenberg, was born on 25 February 1885, in the same room and bed overlooking the Long Walk at Windsor, as she had been born in herself nearly twenty-two years earlier. She was named Alice in memory of her grandmother. When she was about four, Alice refused to kiss her great-grandmother's hand. 'Naughty child,' the Queen said in a severe voice, slapping her hand gently. 'Naughty Grandmama,' Alice retorted, returning the slap. Princess Victoria hurriedly removed her.[4]

Although the Queen was fond of small children, sometimes she seemed shy when confronted by them. When she was seventy-five, she met Victor Mallet, then a month off his second birthday. Victor was the son of her lady-in-waiting, Marie Mallet, and one of her many godsons. She described the 'audience', at which she introduced Victor in his smart brown velvet blouse, muslin collar and ruffs, to kiss her hand and answer 'Good morning Queen', boldly. He was 'charmed at once by the Queen's beaming smile', as she announced that she had a little present for him. On a low table was a miniature landau drawn by a pair of grey horses, gaily painted and lined with blue satin. His eyes grew large as he murmured 'Gee-gees', running excitedly to the table. While his mother and the Queen were talking, his eye wandered round the room and he suddenly pointed to a picture by Landseer of one of the Prince Consort's greyhounds, murmuring 'Bootiful dog'. No courtier, his mother commented approvingly, could have spoken better. After further conversation, she touched her electric bell to signify the audience was at an end. 'Thank-oo kind Queen,' Victor piped up when prompted by his mother, and kissed hands. It was with some difficulty that Marie persuaded her son to leave the room with her.[5]

Well-behaved children were a delight to the Queen, but bad manners were never tolerated. Entering a room at Windsor one day, she saw movement behind the curtains. Tearing them open, she found a page-boy evidently sucking a sweet. 'You horrid small boy!' she snapped, smacking his cheek. A saliva-covered bull's-eye promptly shot across the floor.[6]

The experiences at court of the son of John Dalton, now Canon of St George's, Windsor, left their mark on him. The tutor to the Prince of Wales's sons, who remained a bachelor well into his forties, had married Catharine Evan Thomas in 1886. The following year their son Hugh was born at the family home, The Gnoll, a country mansion near Neath, Glamorgan, and brought up at The Cloisters, near St George's Chapel, Windsor. One of his godparents was Prince Albert Victor, who was in Denmark when the christening took place, but sent a set of drinking cups bought in Copenhagen as a present for his little godson: 'I think they ought to come in useful when my Godson grows older as I used to have the same kind of cups for drinking out of as a child.'[7]

One of Hugh Dalton's first memories, he claimed, was being wheeled in a pram by his nurse down the Long Walk, at Windsor, between lines of elm trees. Seeing a woman picking up odds and ends of firewood, he pointed at her, saying, 'Look, there's a lady picking up sticks!' The nurse who, he said, was 'well trained in the stiff class structure of our society', retorted, 'That's not a lady. That's only an old woman.' At tea, he was presented to a titled visitor. 'Come and say "how-do-you-do" to this lady,' his mother instructed. 'You're not a lady,' he snapped at the visitor, 'you're only an old woman.'[8] From that incident, he averred, dated his sense of social equality.

At the age of four Hugh attended a Christmas party at Windsor Castle as, he says, one of 'hundreds', seated at long tables. Queen Victoria entered with a lady-in-waiting, and the children were all called to attention, ordered to stand up and stop eating. The Queen passed slowly, evidently told by the lady the name of each child, saying a few words to all in turn. When she came to Hugh she looked at his plate, which he had just filled generously.

'What a lot of grapes you've got,' she remarked with some asperity.

'Yes, Queen,' he replied shrilly.

'I expect you'd like me to go away, so that you can eat all those grapes.'

'Yes, Queen.'

She turned to the lady-in-waiting and said crossly, 'What a loud voice that child has, just like his father!'[9] Nobody, it was said, could ever fall asleep during his sermons.

In his memoirs Hugh Dalton looked back on his royal surroundings with ill-concealed distaste. He had no affection for royalty, partly as they offended his 'sense of social equality', and partly as the royal family had the first claim on his father's affections. In particular, the Canon was too devoted to the development and welfare of Princes Albert Victor and George of Wales, and his own family – particularly his son – paid the price. The former died when

Hugh was only four, but George, created Duke of York a few months after his brother's death, treated Hugh with 'only well-trained politeness' when he was an adult. As King, George V once had to receive father and son together, and afterwards turned to the Canon, ordering him never to bring that anarchist son of his near him again.

John Dalton's second child was stillborn, and his third was a daughter, named Alexandra Mary, always 'Georgie' in the family after the Duke of York who was her godfather. Her father was so disappointed at not having another son that when he was given the news he turned on his heels in disgust and left the room. He never took more than a grudging interest in his son and daughter, who bore the scars throughout childhood. Sad to say, this shared parental coldness did not bring them any closer. As a boy Hugh disliked his sister, bullying and teasing her persistently. The mutual antipathy lasted throughout their lives.*

Princess Ena was a special favourite at court. Queen Victoria doted on her, and Henry was especially proud of his fair-haired daughter. He spent more time with their children than Beatrice,

---

*Canon John Dalton died in 1931 and his wife in 1944. By this time, Hugh was a Labour Member of Parliament and senior minister in the wartime government, while Georgie, a lifelong Conservative, was married to Sir John Forbes Watson, Director of the Confederation of British Employers. The jewellery and ornaments were left to her, and private papers to Hugh, but both had an equal claim to their mother's possessions. They quarrelled in the arbitrating presence of a representative of the Public Trustees, and Hugh suggested that royal items of obvious financial value could be sold as long as they lacked the royal cipher. He then waved a contemptuous hand over the rest and boomed at his sister: 'You can have the bloody lot!'[10]

King George VI was so angry at hearing that Hugh Dalton had sold gifts originally presented by members of his family, that he asked for any royal gifts still in the possession of the Forbes Watson family to be returned forthwith. Such was the evidence of Georgie's daughter Heather, who was at boarding school. (She presumably heard about the matter from her mother, whose fury doubtless coloured her retelling of events). As a minister, Hugh was no more popular with his sovereign than he had been with his sovereign's father. King George VI once told the Labour leader Hugh Gaitskell that he was 'the only one of your people' he could not abide.

who seemed curiously unmaternal. Perhaps she had been so used to acting as an unofficial honorary secretary and companion to her mother that old habits died hard. Henry it was who could be relied on to make time to attend to his children's games and lessons. From time to time he went sailing abroad, as a safety valve from the boredom of life at his mother-in-law's court. When he returned after these trips he always brought back presents for his children. From Seville, he brought Ena a fan when she was five. Her first link with the country of which she would one day be Queen Consort, she treasured it throughout her life.

Though Queen Victoria adored her Battenberg grandchildren, there was no question of her granting them any licence not accorded to the others. On wet days at Windsor they had to stay indoors, and were not allowed to play the piano or sing, or make a noise. In order to keep boredom at bay, they devised a game called 'Christian martyrs', in which they prowled around the rooms looking for each other, then inflicted pain on their victim, who was not allowed to make a noise.

As the only girl with three brothers, Ena longed to take part in the boys' games and activities. Forbidden to climb a high tree her brothers used to enjoy, she would sit sobbing underneath, 'I can *do* it. I can *do* it. And I fall softer than they do.'[11]

Often disobedient, she came in for her fair share of punishment. One day the governess tied her hands together with rope, and connected it to the outside knob of the door. Anyone passing could see her, and she was terrified the Queen would come past. Soon the Prime Minister, Lord Salisbury, came on his way to see the Queen on official business. 'Surely you must have stolen the Crown Jewels to be punished like this?' he asked her gravely. Had she been impertinent? She could not remember. Laughing good-naturedly at her plight, he untied the rope.[12]

Ena was a bright, lively child, with a tendency to answer back that irked her grandmother. Before the Duke of York's wedding in June 1893, she was warned to be quiet in church, as nobody was meant to talk through. Everything was fine until the Archbishop began to read the service, only to be interrupted by a shrill five-year-old voice calling out, 'But, Mummy, *that* man is talking.'[13] Queen Victoria, she thought, never seemed to understand children, and asked them so many questions that they became confused. She resented the fact that she and her brothers, being family residents, were nearly always given 'dull nursery meals', while visiting children were treated to eclairs and ices. Once she was moved to make her own defiant protest, saying clearly as her grace, 'Thank God for my dull dinner', much to the Queen's anger.[14]

At the age of six Ena had an accident when her pony fell and rolled on top of her. Beatrice saw the groom leading her back by the hand, noticed she was crying, and soon had her safely in bed. The first doctor summoned suggested that their might have been some indication of suffusion of blood on the brain, and a second doctor was called for. Fortunately, there was no injury to the spine.

Nevertheless, it was a time of grave anxiety. 'You will be glad to hear that dear little Ena is nearly quite herself again,' Beatrice wrote to a friend at court (6 March 1894), '& I hope soon every trace of the terrible accident will have disappeared. We can never be thankful enough for her merciful perseverance, but we passed through terrible days of suspense and adversity.'[15]

Even more suspense and adversity was to touch the Battenbergs less than two years later. Chafing at the emptiness of life in his new home, Henry volunteered to serve in the Ashanti campaign in Africa in 1895. Only with the greatest reluctance did his wife and mother-in-law let him go. They never saw him again, for in January 1896 he contracted malaria and died on his way home. To preserve his body on its last sad journey through the tropical heat, it was placed in a tank made from biscuit tins and filled with rum. When his children heard about it, Prince Alexander recalled in later life, they all suffered from nightmares for weeks.

The children attended the funeral at Whippingham Church, near Osborne. Alexander walked between his uncles, the Prince of Wales and the Duke of Connaught, while the other three rode in the Queen's carriage with their mother and grandmother.

It was not the only shadow they had to face. Leopold, named after the short-lived haemophiliac uncle whom he had never known, suffered from the same condition. He too was a source of endless cosseting and anxiety to the elder generation, who feared correctly that he too would not live to a great age. Beatrice, wrote Marie Mallet, 'tries to cultivate the maternal instinct – she loses so much. Leopold is an angel child, so sweet and attractive. He pines for someone to cling to – he wants petting and spoiling.'[16] Beatrice found it difficult to pet and spoil her children, and the gap was filled to some extent by ladies-in-waiting, Marie Mallet herself and Louisa, Countess of Antrim.

For the first few years, the children were educated by nannies. In March 1899 Mr Theobald was employed as tutor to teach the boys. He gained their confidence quickly, and he soon established a ready rapport with them. Maurice was a mischievous youngster, and his first surviving letter, written to Mr Theobald after he had accompanied Beatrice, Leopold and the Queen to Nice that spring, remarked, 'I hope you were very sick on the ship and I hope Leopold has bullied you as much as he can on the train. I want to know if you have given Leopold a lot of arithmetic. I am glad you are not here as I miss your smacks much.' It was signed 'your noisy Maurice'.[17]

Queen Victoria's first great-grandchild, Princess Feodora of Saxe-Meiningen, was born in May 1879, the only child of her eldest granddaughter Princess Charlotte of Prussia. Though she always took a keen interest in her numerous descendants, the great-grandchildren to whom she was closest and most interested were inevitably the grandchildren of her son and heir, the Prince of Wales.

In May 1890 the Queen created his elder son, Prince Albert Victor, Duke of Clarence and Avondale. As the next sovereign but one, he did not look like a promising future King. He had inherited his father's vices (and perhaps more) without his abilities or strength of character. Easy-going to the point of imbecility, chronically slow, prematurely deaf like his mother, he was probably dyslexic, and perhaps also a sufferer from porphyria, a more virulent form of which was mistakenly diagnosed as insanity in its most famous and unfortunate victim, his great-great-grandfather King George III. He was said to have been involved in various scandals, including a homosexual brothel in Cleveland Place which was raided by the police, and in the Jack the Ripper murders in 1888. Though such rumours were based on hearsay, it was evident to the elder generation that his salvation lay in a steady wife who would hopefully be the making of him. An engagement between him and the obedient Princess May of Teck was carefully arranged in December 1891. Six weeks later he succumbed to a severe epidemic of influenza which had ravaged the country that Christmas.

The following year his sole surviving brother George, recently created Duke of York, proposed to May, and they were married in July 1893. Eleven months later, on 23 June 1894, the Duchess of York gave birth to the first of six children. Queen Victoria made a special visit to White Lodge, Richmond, to see her great-grandson. With pride she wrote to Vicky, now the widowed Empress Frederick, that 'it has never happened in this country that there should be three direct heirs as well as the sovereign alive'.[18]

To the public the child was always known as Prince Edward, though *en famille* called by the last of his seven Christian names, David. His brother was born at York Cottage on the Sandringham estate on 14 December 1895, the anniversary of double tragedy – the deaths of the Prince Consort and Princess Alice. 'Grandmama was rather distressed,' the Prince of Wales told his son, but he himself trusted that the young prince's birth would 'break the spell' of the unlucky date. It would be tactful, he suggested, to invite Queen Victoria to be the baby's godmother, and to call him Albert.*

The Duke of York and his elder brother had experienced the swing of the pendulum. Notwithstanding their exalted rank, they had enjoyed an upbringing which was in some respects very carefree – considerably more so than that of their father. For the two Princes born in 1894 and 1895, the pendulum swung back again, and they suffered the customary fate of most upper-class children of the time. Their existence was supervised by nurses, and much depended not on their parents so much as on the character and temperament of their nannies, whom they saw much more frequently. Busy as they had been with state matters, Queen Victoria and Prince Albert had always made time to keep a careful eye on their eldest children and the women appointed to look after them, in addition to having the additional counsel of Baron Stockmar, and the Prince and Princess of Wales had likewise been the most devoted of mothers and fathers.

Most Victorian children were less fortunate, and the young Yorks were no exception. Like so many of their contemporaries, their

---

*He was christened Albert Frederick Arthur George, but known by family and public alike as Prince Albert (and from 1920, Duke of York) until his accession to the throne as King George VI in 1936.

parents were at first sadly unaware of what went on out of sight. The children were kept in the nursery, brought down, washed, brushed, and dressed in their best everyday clothes at teatime for perhaps one hour of the twenty-four. For the rest of their waking hours, they were at the mercy of their nurses or governesses. The Yorks' first nurse was dismissed for being rude to the Duchess of Teck. The second was sadistic and incompetent. She showed a marked preference for Edward, to whom her devotion was so fanatical that, in order to demonstrate the superiority of her power over him to that of his parents, she would twist and pinch his arm before bringing him into the drawing-room. As a result a sobbing, bawling infant was quickly removed from the room before further embarrassment was inflicted upon them.

By way of contrast, Albert was ignored to a degree which bordered on neglect. He was usually given his afternoon bottle while being driven around in a C-spring victoria, which gave a notoriously bumpy ride comparable to a rough Channel crossing. Soon he developed chronic stomach trouble, resulting in the gastric problems which plagued him as a young man. The under-nurse Mrs Charlotte Bill, known as 'Lalla' by the children, was shocked when the nurse snatched the bowl away from him at meals, declaring that he had had enough for one day.

At length Mrs Bill could take this woman's ill-treatment of the infants no longer. Although worried that if she spoke out the nurse would vent her anger on them, she told the housekeeper everything. On investigation, it was established that the woman had not had a day off for three years, that she was unable to have children and had been deserted by her husband, and was suffering from frustrated and warped maternal instincts. She was dismissed, and her place was taken by the more understanding Mrs Bill.

Albert's birth was followed by that of a sister, born on 25 April 1897, named Mary. She was something of a tomboy and, as the only girl among an eventual crowd of boys, inclined to be spoilt. Her disciplinarian father treated her far more leniently than her brothers, though she was easily embarrassed and his teasing often made her blush. Even so, fortunate was the only Princess in a gang of brothers. The future Crown Prince William of Germany would recall that his sister, Victoria Louise, was the only one of the family of seven who succeeded during childhood in winning a place in the heart of their father, Emperor William II. He and his brothers were treated with severity. For example, when they entered his study, they had to hold their hands behind them lest they knock anything off the tables.

The Duke and Duchess of York were evidently happy to accept the principle that children should never be heard and only seen on appropriate and carefully regulated occasions. A swing door was put across the passage on the first floor beyond the Duke and Duchess's bedrooms and those of the household, and beyond it two small, simply furnished rooms were designated for the children. One was the 'day nursery', where the children ate, played and had their first lessons. In her old age, Mrs Bill reminisced on her days of employment at York Cottage. The day nursery, she declared, was only about half the size of what Prince Edward – by then Duke of Windsor – called 'her modest suburban living-room'. 'There was very little room for toys in it,' she told him. 'You had only one small-sized rocking horse. Perhaps it was a good thing your sister didn't go for dolls. They would have cluttered up the place terribly.'[19]

The 'night nursery' was slightly larger. Here the children slept with a nurse, and had their baths in round tin tubs filled with hot water from cans brought by servants from the cellar. Through the windows they could look out over the pond at Sandringham, with its small island almost smothered with brambles reached by a bridge, to the park where small web-antlered Japanese deer grazed. They would lie in bed listening to the wild duck on the pond at dawn and at dusk, the cooing of the wood pigeons in the trees of the park, and sometimes the call of their grandfather's cock-pheasants in the woods.

As babies the children had to wear very thick clothing. Their first clothes were 'layers of long flowing robes of cambric and muslin and lace'.[20] The weight of such garments was tiring to the right arm, however strong, of the nurse who had to carry them, as well as to the babies themselves. At that time it was the rule that a nurse had to carry the baby in her arms for the first three months of his or her life, and if she did not or could not do so, she was adjudged not fit to do her job. Edward put this down to a superstition that the jolting of a perambulator would be harmful to the baby.

Prince George, Duke of York and later Prince of Wales, was never the devoted, free and easy father that his own father had been. He claimed that he was devoted to children, and 'get on with them like a house on fire'. In practice, this generally meant other people's children, not least his nephews and nieces. With his own youngsters, he was a model father – to a point. When they were babies, he sometimes helped to bathe them – 'I make a very good lap' – and when they were old enough he taught them to handle a gun or a fishing rod.

None the less, once they were past the baby stage he was something of a martinet. According to his first biographer, John Gore, 'his banter embarrassed and silenced them and he had a way of asking what they had been doing and then supplying chaffing answers before the little boys could supply their own words'.[21]

'Now that you are five years old,' he wrote to Prince Albert on the latter's birthday in December 1900, 'I hope you will always try & be obedient & do at once what you are told, as you will find it will come much easier to you the sooner you begin. I always tried to do this when I was your age & found it made me much happier.'[22] Even the Prince Consort, so long regarded as the personification of pedantic fatherhood, never subjected his eldest son to such lofty missives at such an early age.

When they were older the Duchess of York would sit in the drawing-room entertaining the children. Sometimes she would summon them round the card table to play an educational game, for example one with the counties of England. With a lady-in-waiting at the piano, she would teach the two elder boys songs from an old community song book, like 'Swanee River', 'Funiculi, Funicula', 'The Camptown Races', and 'Clementine'.

It was part of the Duchess's routine to rest in her boudoir for the hour before dinner. At 6.30 every evening, the children were called in from the schoolroom. She would be in her negligée resting on the sofa, with her workbox on the lower shelf of a two-tiered table beside her, the top of which was covered with miniature trinkets. They would come and sit near her while she read to them, often royal history. In his later years, Edward looked on this domestic scene with fond affection. 'Her soft voice, her cultivated mind, the cosy room overflowing with personal treasures were all inseparable ingredients of the happiness associated with this last hour of a child's day.'[23] The Duke never lingered over his tea in the drawing-room, preferring to retire to his study (rather grandly known as 'the library'), where he would read *The Times*, catch up with his correspondence, write up his game book or occupy himself with his stamp collection until dinner was ready.

Being practical by nature, and like most Victorian parents keen to discourage idleness among her children, the Duchess taught them how to make woollen comforters for one of her charities. Each child was handed a wooden ring fitted with upright brass pegs. While she read, they looped the wool yarn around each peg, eventually forming a five-foot long scarf. She was not a particularly maternal woman, finding the whole progress of pregnancy and childbearing distasteful and embarrassing. She did not enjoy bathing them like their grandmothers did. Uninterested in babies, like her husband she had no automatic or spontaneous understanding of a child's mind, and expected them to behave like miniature adults. She spoke of finding Prince Edward 'jumpy' at the age of two, or 'in a delicious frame of mind . . . I really believe he begins to like me at last, he is most civil to me'.[24] Such terms seem distinctly distant about one's own child.

Nevertheless, Edward recalled, she was very proud of her children: 'everything that happened to each one was of the utmost importance to her'.[25] With the birth of each baby, she followed the contemporary custom of starting an album in which she carefully recorded each progressive stage of childhood, including the dates on which a first tooth was cut, or first step was taken, and a lock of hair inserted on the day of the first haircut.

The children's happiest childhood memories were of the times when they were alone with their mother at Frogmore or Abergeldie, while their father was away shooting in the Midlands or yachting at Cowes. Her husband was nevertheless a repressive influence on her, and she backed him up in all matters of discipline relating to the children. All the same, her eldest son recalled, 'she never failed to take our side whenever in her judgement he was being too harsh with us'.[26]

One more occupant of the Yorks' nursery was born during Queen Victoria's lifetime, a third son, who was named Henry. He arrived on 31 March 1900. One of the last photographs of Queen

Victoria, taken in the summer of 1900, showed her sitting on the lawn at Osborne House apparently holding Henry on her lap, and surrounded by his brothers and sister. Discreetly hidden from the camera lens was Mrs Bill, crouching behind to support the baby with her own arm, as the Queen was so frail that she was afraid of dropping him. The great-grandchildren were terrified by the elderly little lady in a black bombazine dress or, possibly, her Indian servants (or maybe a combination of both). In particular the two elder boys used to cry from nerves whenever they were taken to Windsor or Osborne to see her, and she would ask the Duchess of York with some irritation 'what she had done now', or scold Mrs Bill. 'You had to mind your step with Queen Victoria,' the latter recalled. Perhaps she was almost as much in awe of her sovereign as the infants themselves.

At this time the British Empire was locked in a struggle with the Boers in South Africa. Edward's first clear memories of world events were of the war, as for a time after the outbreak of hostilities in October 1899, little else was talked about in the family. His three uncles on his mother's side were all on active service with their regiments; their letters from the front were read aloud to the children, and in the more sensational newspapers favoured by the nurses to which they had access (without full parental approval, it may be supposed), they would pore over artists' sketches of battles which showed Highlanders dying on the barbed wire in front of Magersfontein, or the capture of Royal Horse Artillery guns. When they were taken for walks in Hyde Park, they would stop to watch troops drilling on the grass, and a drive through the city streets often brought them within view of columns of khaki-clad troops with wide-brimmed hats on their way to the front, swinging along behind brass bands playing patriotic songs of the day such as 'Soldiers of the Queen' or 'Tommy Atkins'. One spring evening when they were staying at Balmoral, a great bonfire was lit by the Queen's Highland retainers on top of the hill above the castle, in celebration of one of the British victories in South Africa.

Meanwhile, growing up as an almost exact contemporary of the Prince of Wales's children was another Prince destined to have a considerable influence on public life during the century: His

Serene Highness Prince Louis Francis of Battenberg. Born at Frogmore House on 25 June 1900, the fourth child and second son of Prince Louis and the former Princess Victoria of Hesse, he was the last of Queen Victoria's great-grandchildren to be born during her lifetime. He was christened Louis Francis Albert Victor Nicholas, in the drawing-room at Frogmore on 17 July.

Though the Queen was increasingly frail and almost blind by now, she insisted on holding the baby throughout the ceremony evidently with help. She was his godmother and, although he knocked her spectacles off with one hand and pulled at her veil with the other, she noted afterwards that the 'beautiful large child . . . behaved very well'. It was a very hot day, and to try to bring down the temperature of the room, a bucket of ice was put under one of the chairs. The unfortunate Dean of Windsor sat on the chair, chilled his legs, and the result for him was a serious sciatic inflammation. Afterwards he could only walk with the aid of a stick.

In January 1901 the York children were at York Cottage, quarantined in the nursery for German measles. The Duke and Duchess of York had gone to London for a reception for Lord Roberts, Commander-in-Chief of the British forces in South Africa, when they were informed by the Prince of Wales that Queen Victoria had had a slight stroke at Osborne. Her condition was not considered dangerous at first, and the Duke and Duchess returned to Sandringham for the last days of the shooting season. The children were not allowed to see them as they were still in quarantine. A day or two later they were told that their parents had gone to Osborne, as 'Gangan' was dying.

Surrounded by most of her surviving children and many of her grandchildren, she passed away on 22 January. The Duke of York, now heir to the throne, promptly went down with German measles, and the Duchess remained behind to nurse him. She asked her mother-in-law, now Queen Alexandra, to arrange for the three elder children to see the funeral service in St George's Chapel, Windsor, and her interment at Frogmore. They were, however, spared a last sight of their great-grandmother's body laid out at Osborne before being placed in the coffin. Their five-year-old cousin, Princess Elizabeth of Hesse, was brought in to see her. Peering solemnly, she whispered, 'But I don't see the wings.'[27]

On the bitterly cold afternoon of 2 February, the three small

Yorks stood among the sorrowful company of kings, princes and dignitaries for the obsequies. Prince Edward's memories were of 'the piercing cold, the interminable waits, and of feeling very lost among scores of sorrowing grown up relatives, solemn Princes in varied uniforms, and Princesses sobbing behind heavy crêpe veils.'[28] He must have looked 'very lost', for his aunt Princess Charles of Denmark noticed Princess Elizabeth, 'who took him under her protection and held him most of the time round his neck. They looked such a delightful little couple!'[29]

8

'Innate boisterousness'

King Edward VII had been on the throne for barely two months when, on 16 March 1901, the Duke and Duchess of York sailed from Portsmouth for a visit to Australia. For almost eight blissful months, the young Yorks were allowed a respite from their parents' strict regime. King Edward and Queen Alexandra had never been strict parents as Prince and Princess of Wales, and with the cares of sovereignty weighing heavily on them, they found light relief in looking after and spoiling the youngsters whom the Queen called 'the Georgiepets'. She would let her grandsons pour salt and pepper into her glass, and to their delight drink the result, pretending to be unaware of what they had done. One day the King told Edward to stop interrupting him, then asked what he wanted to say. The boy gleefully pointed out that he had wished to warn him of a slug on his lettuce, but it was too late as he had eaten it now.

If the superimposition of four noisy children upon the Royal Household during their parents' absence was ever a nuisance, their grandparents never let them know it, Edward recalled. 'On the contrary, they encouraged our innate boisterousness to such an extent that the quiet routine of York Cottage suffered a brief but harmless setback.'[1]

For about a year, their lessons had been supervised by a lady from Alsace, Mlle Helen Bricka, who had taught the adolescent Duchess of York. In those days, she had been a satisfactory governess for a girl of finishing-school age. However, now plump and elderly, she found her old pupil's restless little boys more than a handful. Their grandfather, now their King, remembered his schoolroom days with a shudder, and their grandmother never thought that lessons were more important than a happy childhood. If there were no dignitaries guesting at lunch, they liked to have the children romping around in the dining-room at Buckingham Palace, regardless of the fact that Mlle Bricka was waiting upstairs impatiently, French and German primers at the ready. If she entered the dining-room timidly to warn the children that they were a little late for their afternoon lesson, Queen Alexandra would gently wave her away, while King Edward would ask for them to stay a little longer, and they would be sent upstairs presently. One could hardly argue with the King. When the family went on a two-week stay to Sandringham, Mlle Bricka was left behind in London 'lest she should spoil the fun'.

The Duchess of York wrote to express her irritation, but the Queen defended their decision on the grounds that Dr Laking had particularly asked that Edward should be left more with his brothers and sister for a while, 'as we *all* noticed *how* precautious [*sic*] & *old-fashioned* he was getting – & quite the *ways* of *a "single child"*'! which wld make him ultimately a "tiresome child" – laying down the law & thinking himself far superior to the younger ones.'[2] His education, she assured her daughter-in-law, had not been neglected.

The parents might be out of sight, but they were not out of mind. The Duke of York had left strict instructions that the two elder sons must write regularly to their parents. In addition to his own replies, long and instructive letters were written to the Princes from various ports of call by Walter Jones, the village schoolmaster of Sandringham, an old friend of the Duke from younger days, whom he had attached to his suite.

On 1 November the Duke and Duchess returned to Portsmouth. Before taking the children to meet their parents, King Edward warned them gravely that they had been exposed for a time to the fierce tropical sun, and their skins would have probably turned black. They were horrified, until a glance at their parents in the distance proved that Grandpa had been teasing them.

The cheerful, undisciplined children who greeted the Duke and Duchess – created Prince and Princess of Wales eight days later, on the King's sixtieth birthday – now needed a course of 'character moulding'. To their parents it was evident that Princes Edward and Albert could no longer stay in the nursery under feminine supervision.

On New Year's Day 1902 they were told that Frederick Finch would wake them up the following morning, and thenceforth they would be under his care. Mr Finch had entered the family's service three years earlier as nursery footman. He had brought the children their meals, carried the bathwater, and performed all the other heavy chores of the nursery. Now he performed the duties of a nanny: he polished his young charges' shoes, nursed them, made sure they scrubbed their hands and faces properly, and heard their prayers every morning and evening.

Finch was a firm but not unreasonable disciplinarian. One afternoon when the young Mary was meant to be taking a nap, Edward went into the nursery and started fooling around. A harassed Mrs Bill, unable to control him, eventually went into Finch's room to tell him bluntly that 'that boy' was impossible, and if he did not give him a thrashing she would. Finch promptly fetched the Prince and spanked him soundly, to the accompaniment of yells more out of hurt pride than physical pain. As Finch left, Edward shouted that he would 'get even' with him and tell his father. In the end, the Princess of Wales was told. She scolded her son for his misbehaviour, and also for being so foolish as to suppose that a servant had no right to punish him. Penitently, he was sent to apologize to Finch for being such a nuisance.

1902 was a busy year for the family, for they spent most of the spring preparing for King Edward VII's Coronation, which was to take place on 26 June. Henry Hansell, a former master from Eton and one-time tutor to Prince Arthur of Connaught, had recently been appointed to supervise the boys' education. He took advantage of impending events to try to bring their history lessons to life. After explaining to them the symbolism of the Coronation service and the meaning of all the pageantry, he took them around the city and showed them round Westminster Abbey, the Houses of Parliament, St Paul's Cathedral and other famous landmarks. If his painstaking expositions of ceremony and pageantry rather went over their heads, they never tired of seeing colourfully decorated stands in the streets, and large contingents of troops in the main parks.

The Coronation was postponed when the King was taken ill three days before the ceremony was scheduled, and underwent an emergency operation for appendicitis. An impatient but slimmer and fitter King was crowned at Westminster Abbey on 9 August. Before leaving Buckingham Palace for the abbey that morning, his grandchildren were speechless as they gazed at him in his finery with awe. 'Good morning children, am I not a funny-looking old man?' he asked them genially, keen to break the ice.

King Edward's love of small children was legendary. Although he spared himself little in affairs of state during his nine-year reign, he was always at ease in the company of youngsters, whether they were his own family or the children of courtiers.

One particular favourite was Sonia, the little girl of his last mistress and trusted confidante, Alice Keppel. Born in 1900, the year before his accession to the throne, Sonia's earliest memories were of being dressed up by her nanny and given firm injunctions to be sure to curtsy to the King. Shyly, she hardly dared to raise her eyes above the gentlemen's midriffs, and she sometimes curtsied to Sir Ernest Cassel, the similarly wide-girthed Jewish banker and close friend of the King, by mistake.

The King allowed Sonia to call him 'Kingy', and when he came to tea with her mother, a special game was devised. With a fine disregard for the condition of his trousers, she recalled, he invited her to put two bits of bread and butter, the latter side down, side by side down his leg. 'Then, bets of a penny each were made (my bet provided by Mamma) and the winning piece of bread and butter depended, of course, on which was the more buttery. The excitment was intense while the contest was on. Sometimes he won, sometimes I did. Although the owner of a Derby winner, Kingy's enthusiasm seemed delightfully unaffected by the quality of his bets.'[3]

The lives of the Prince of Wales's children no longer revolved around York Cottage. As Prince of Wales, their father was granted two additional residences, Frogmore, at Home Park, Windsor, and Abergeldie, at Balmoral. Frogmore, where they stayed for the first time in the weeks leading up to the Coronation, had little in the way of modern conveniences, and lacked electric light and modern heating. All the same, it provided the children with additional outdoor premises to play in, especially the limitless expanse of the Great Park, and the vast roof of the castle itself, all the more fascinating as it was officially forbidden territory.

To the younger generation Frogmore, like Osborne (which the King handed over to the Royal Navy as a training college shortly after Queen Victoria's death), had the air of a family necropolis.

Among the marble busts and lifesize statues that lined the corridors was one of Edward, Duke of Kent. The boys were fascinated by it because their great-great-grandfather looked exactly like one of their parents' footmen, Mr Smithson. The resemblance became even more pronounced after they placed Smithson's off-duty cloth check cap on the head of the bust. They could not resist inviting their mother to come and look. Although much amused, she lectured them gently on the impropriety of making fun of one of their illustrious ancestors, and also on holding up one of their servants to ridicule. Was she afraid that jokes might lead to rumours about his ancestry? Where the 'ridicule' argument was concerned, they knew better. One day when she was out, they put the cap on the bust again, and called Smithson to see. Far from being offended, he beamed with pleasure, agreed the likeness was striking, and not long afterwards the youngsters noticed him standing admiringly before the bust.

After the excitement of the Coronation, the Prince and Princess of Wales took their family to Abergeldie for the summer. Like previous royal generations, the children were fascinated by the wild Deeside scenery, 'in sharp contrast to the noble, well-tended beauty of Windsor and the wooded tranquillity of Sandringham; and the gurgling of the swift-running river splashing over the granite boulders scattered along the length of its shallow bed filled the rooms of the old house with a sound I [Prince Edward] loved to hear.'[4]

While their father spent his days making the most of the season's sport, their mother took them for carriage rides along the forest roads with a picnic tea that they brought in a basket and spread out on the heather in some suitably picturesque spot, when weather permitted. Unfortunately the elements were not on their side in Scotland that summer. They had arrived at Abergeldie in pelting rain, which continued for several days on end. The Princess of Wales, expecting a fifth child at the end of the year, was tired and exhausted after the festivities in London. She did not share her in-laws' enthusiasm for Balmoral, and the damp dreary days did nothing to raise her drooping spirits. With his customary sense of slightly barbed humour, her husband remarked lightly that he would soon have a regiment, not a family.

With the end of that eventful summer came their return to York Cottage, and for the two elder boys, the beginning of their serious education. According to Prince Edward, Mr Hansell 'combined a mild scholarship with a muscular Christianity, accentuated by tweeds and an ever-present pipe'.[5] He took his breakfast and lunch with the boys every day, but dined with their parents and members of the household in the evening.

Like Birch and Gibbs before him, he thought the boys should have the chance to grow up in a normal, more rigorously competitive environment with others of their own age. When his suggestion that the Princes should go to preparatory school was vetoed, he attempted to create a schoolroom atmosphere in a room on the second floor at York Cottage. A classroom was fitted with two standard desks, a blackboard, a set of wall maps, and shelves stocked with the standard text books in arithmetic, history and grammar. After being woken by Mr Finch at 7.00 a.m., they would be at their desks from 7.30 to 8.15 a.m. for preparation, or homework. Breakfast was followed by further preparation from 9.00 a.m. to 1.00 p.m. (with an hour's break for play), then lunch, followed by a walk in the woods or the chance to kick a football around. Between tea and supper there were lessons. Sometimes informal and immature football matches would be organized by Hansell, the Princes being joined by boys from the village school.

The educational regime laid down for the Princes sounds almost like a carbon copy of that practised by Birch and Gibbs for King Edward VII as a boy and his late brother Alfred.* If Hansell expected them to be shining paragons of virtue, he was disappointed. They were disobedient, enjoyed fooling around, became frustrated when their work seemed difficult; in short, they were wearisomely normal. His weekly, sometimes daily, reports to the Prince of Wales make predictable reading. 'Both boys must give a *readier* obedience,' he noted solemnly on 20 September 1902. 'I often describe them to myself as obedient boys at the second time of asking.' Fisticuffs were common, as shown in a report of 16 January 1904: 'I am very sorry to say that Prince Albert has caused two painful scenes in his bedroom this week. On

---

*Prince Alfred, Duke of Edinburgh, had succeeded his uncle Ernest as Duke of Saxe-Coburg Gotha in 1893 and died in July 1900, predeceasing his mother by nearly six months.

the second occasion I understand that he narrowly escaped giving his brother a very severe kick, it being absolutely unprovoked & Finch being engaged in helping Prince Edward at the time.'[6]

Mr Hansell assumed the 'position' of headmaster, and secured the services of a small teaching staff under him. Mr Walter Jones helped to organize games, as well as taking the boys for walks in the Norfolk countryside and passing on his love of local flora and fauna. M. Hua, who had taught (or tried to teach) the young Prince George of Wales French, and later became a master at Eton, and Professor Oswald, both taught languages, while Mr Martin David, a mathematics master at Tonbridge School, looked after the other essential subjects. Professor Oswald evidently had little sense of discipline. When he complained to the Prince of Wales of Albert's inattention and was asked for details, he explained with embarrassment that not only did His Royal Highness not pay attention, but when scolded just pulled his beard.

All the assistant masters were encouraged to write any details of bad work or misconduct in a report book, which Mr Hansell would note and deal with accordingly. Lapses on the boys' part resulted in a summons, usually delivered by a footman, that 'His Royal Highness wishes to see you in the Library.' The library was regarded as their father's 'Captain's Cabin'. Sometimes the message was delivered merely because he wanted to show the children some new stamps he had just acquired and was particularly pleased about, or to make them a present of some curio that he had obtained on his travels. More often than not, though, it foretold a dressing-down. No words were more calculated to strike terror into their hearts than the announcement that they were wanted in the library.

The children saw few of their contemporaries, except in the rare games of cricket and football. When Edward was nearly nine, the Princess of Wales decided to remedy the situation. While they were at York House in London, she suggested that they should be taught how to dance. A class of twenty or more boys and girls was organized, with a lady at the piano providing the music, while a very stout yet surprisingly nimble Miss Walsh showed them the steps of the polka, the waltz, and the Highland *schottische*. The boys wore Eton suits, with the girls attired in short dresses pulled tight at the waist with silk sashes, and a bow tied at the back. There was never anything spontaneous about these classes, but 'they lifted us out, if only briefly, from our walled-in-life in London and brought us together with children of our own age'.[7]

Once transferred to the care of Mr Finch, the boys had to observe a strict dress code. Kilts and sailor suits were regarded by the Prince of Wales as the only appropriate dress for children. Even at the age of nine, on a visit to Balmoral, Edward was given constant admonitions in his father's letters: 'Take care and don't spoil [the kilts] at once as they are new. Wear the Balmoral kilt and grey jacket on weekdays and green kilt and black jacket on Sundays. Do not wear the red kilt till I come.'[8]

The Princes were always 'on parade'. If they appeared before him with their Navy lanyards a fraction of an inch out of place, or with their dirks or sporrans awry, there would be an outburst worthy of the quarterdeck of a warship. When one of them was seen with his hands casually stuffed into his trouser pockets, Mrs Bill was immediately ordered to bring her needle and thread to make sure that such slackness would never be possible again.

In every sense of the word, Edward considered, it was 'a buttoned-up childhood'. On occasions when the Princes were forced to wear their starched Eton collars, these invariably cut into their necks, as they were often old and frayed. The idea of one of them appearing in shirt sleeves and an open-necked collar was unthinkable. If they were doing hot work outside, they were allowed to roll up their sleeves, but never loosen their collars or take their coats off. Even with shorts they wore long stockings, 'with never a thought of anything so indelicate as bare knees – except in a kilt'.[9]

In terms of dress, the Prince of Wales's children had far less freedom than earlier generations. Edward looked wistfully at Winterhalter's portraits of his grandfather, as a boy of six wearing a sailor suit with – horror of horrors – his hands deep in his pockets. At Windsor he gazed ruefully at Gainsborough's paintings of King George III's sons wearing blouses wide open at the neck.

Yet there was freedom enough to deal with priggish elder cousins. Ena of Battenberg thoroughly disliked Edward, probably because she suspected that when he was born he had displaced her in Queen Victoria's affections. One day at Sandringham when she was aged sixteen and he ten, she told him angrily that he was 'perfectly horrid', and she wanted 'nothing to do with rude little boys who did not behave themselves'. He apologized, and suggested they should go for a walk together. Prepared to make her peace with him, she agreed, and bent down to look closely at a flower-bed where he said he had something to show her. He promptly dropped a worm down the back of her dress.[10]

At the turn of the century rail and steamship were the chief means of transport. The royal children travelled between Windsor, Sandringham and Balmoral by train, while they crossed the Solent to Osborne in a small steamer from Portsmouth. It was a novelty to sleep on the train to Aberdeen, travelling in a 'bed-carriage' which stretched across the seats, linked for the purpose with a close-fitting stool with an upholstered cushion. Journeys to Wolferton Station, near Sandringham, were 'an enjoyable picnic'. As there were no dining-cars en route, they took a well-stocked luncheon basket, and when the train stopped at a suitable station, they were given coffee from a trolley on the platform. On returning from Sandringham, each guest or member of the household would be supplied with his own luncheon-basket, packed in the royal kitchen. When emptied, the baskets were left on the train at St Pancras, cleaned and washed up by the Great Eastern Railway, and returned to Marlborough House or later to Buckingham Palace.

At home they still drove in horse-drawn carriages – wagonettes as a rule, brakes, dog-carts and pony-carriages. Their childhood coincided with the invention of the 'safety bicycle', a distinct improvement on the rather precarious penny-farthing of the previous generation. Until then, the Prince of Wales's children had to ask their nurse or tutor for a carriage and coachman from the royal stables if they wanted to go any further than the grounds of Windsor or Sandringham. When King Edward VII gave Prince Edward his first bicycle, said the latter, 'my life was transformed'. In no time he and his brothers were virtually living on bicycles outside; they could get away on their own, racing against each other and going for ten-mile rides on the comparatively traffic-free roads. At last they could see something of the world outside the gardens and grounds where they lived, and at their own pace.

At the end of the previous century, the motor-car – or 'horseless carriage' – was introduced. Edward had his first ride in one during the autumn of 1902, on the occasion of the planting of an avenue of trees to commemorate his grandfather's Coronation. The two-mile ride, at a speed of 20 m.p.h., seemed at the time like an adventure that was never to be forgotten.

Almost two years after the accession of King Edward VII, George was born on 20 December 1902. He learnt to read quickly, and soon gave promise of being the most academically minded of the family. He was taught French by Mlle Bricka, and took to it immediately, speaking it better than the rest. Although untidy and reputedly the naughtiest of the family, with his charm he was forgiven more readily than the others.

Some two and a half years later, on 12 July 1905, the youngest son, Prince John, was born. John has been the subject of much misinformed comment, allegedly a skeleton in the royal cupboard, and said to be mentally handicapped. In fact he was normal at birth and his mother recovered rapidly from her confinement. His charm manifested itself in quaint remarks. 'She kissed Papa, *ugly* old man,'[11] he was heard to mutter as a three-year-old on holiday at Abergeldie, when he watched his mother greet his father affectionately after returning from a day's stalking. A well-behaved child, he became Mrs Bill's favourite.

Sadly, he began to have epileptic fits at the age of four, and the doctors could do nothing to help. Nevertheless, at first the seizures were not severe enough to prevent him from taking part in normal family life, though he was watched protectively. He appeared regularly in photographs, on his own and with family groups, for several years. To all outward appearances he seemed quite normal.

Edward was fortunate in suffering from no physical handicaps during childhood. The rest all had knock-knees; Albert was the worst afflicted. To help correct the condition in his case, splints were devised by Sir Francis Laking, his father's physician-in-ordinary. For a while the boy had to wear them for part of the day and night, and though they were painful he accepted them as a necessary evil. One night he wept bitterly, pleading not to have to wear them again. Finch, whose duty it was to see that they were properly adjusted, took pity on him. When Laking reported this act of mercy to the Prince of Wales, he summoned Finch to the library, asked him to explain, then stood up and drew his trousers tight against his legs. 'Look at me,' he barked. 'If that boy grows up to look like this, it will be your fault.'

However, the boy persevered, writing with dogged determination to his mother in February 1904 that he was sitting in an armchair, with his legs in the new splints: 'I have got an invalid table, which is splendid for reading but rather awkward for writing at present. I expect I shall get used to it.'[12] At first Mr Hansell found that in the schoolroom the splints caused his pupil such agony that concentration was severely impaired, but after a while they proved so successful that Laking advised they need only be worn at night. After a while it was found that they had indeed served their purpose.

In addition, Albert was also afflicted with a bad stammer from the age of about seven. Like his stomach disorders, it was to cause him trouble throughout his life, though as a young adult a therapist helped him to keep it under control. Naturally left-handed, he was forced to use the right, resulting in a condition known in psychology as a 'misplaced sinister', which probably affected his speech. Sensitive by nature, easily rebuffed and prone to take his weaknesses and faults to heart too much, he was slower and less articulate by nature than his elder brother, and he was intimidated by his father's regular admonitions. Tongue-tied and less able to answer for himself, he found himself increasingly cut off from his parents, brothers and sister, who outpaced him with their quicker level of repartee.

Driven in upon his own resources, he was prone to spells of dreamy abstraction, during which others – particularly Hansell at lesson-time – found it difficult to make him concentrate, and outbursts of excitement, sometimes exuberant, sometimes of passionate weeping and depression. As a child, like the 'Bertie' of an earlier generation, in his earliest years he probably gave his parents and tutor more difficulty than the others put together.

More than his brothers and sister, he inherited his great-grandmother's abiding love for Scotland. Something about the Highland landscape, the rural tranquillity of the Cairngorms and River Dee, struck a chord in him, and it was noticed that, in Scotland, he shed the inhibitions which hampered him in the more formal routine of life at Sandringham and London.

In 1902 Mrs Bill was put in charge of Henry. Already he was showing signs of the family temper. An unnamed observer recalled being at a family party with tutor and governess at Frogmore House with the Prince of Wales, while the elderly Grand Duchess Augusta of Mecklenburg-Strelitz was staying. Towards the end of the meal a door opened, and a sulky-looking small boy in a stiff white petticoat was pushed in. The Princess of Wales called him to her side and he stood glowering between her and the Grand Duchess. His mother could see that he was 'evidently put out about something', but she tried to soothe him and make him speak politely to her guest. At last the Grand Duchess bent her face down and asked him if he could not say anything to her, would he not at least give her a kiss. He would not. Instead there was the sharp sound as a small hand administered a petulant slap on her cheek.

Mary, now five, was entrusted to the care of Else Korsukawitz. A plump, good-tempered, cheerful German, she became the girl's governess, and Mlle Jose Dussau her tutor. The sharp-tongued Mademoiselle was always ready to reporting any lapses of behaviour on the Princes' part, and no petty misdemeanour that came to her notice went unreported in detail to their parents. Mary, no rebel, cheerfully accepted discipline, and relished conformity – if not teasing. The threat to her high-spirited brothers of 'I'll tell Mama', though rarely carried out, acted as a powerful deterrent. Her greatest passion was for riding, in Hyde Park when in London, in Windsor Great Park when the court was in residence at the castle, but whenever possible in the open countryside around Sandringham.

Mary's history lessons were brought to life by visits to the Tower and Hampton Court, and geography was taught with large-scale models. She also studied French and German, making good progress in both, and great emphasis was placed on her deportment. A keen botanist, she made and developed a collection of plants and seaweed indigenous to the Sandringham area. She took cheerfully to her lessons. 'What a pity it's not Mary,' her eldest brother was once reported to have said when reminded of his destiny, 'she is far cleverer than I am.'[13]

After a morning of lessons she took her lunch at 1.00 p.m. with Mrs Bill, Finch, and one of the tutors, then did sewing and painting for an hour. She became proficient with the needle, starting with making clothes for her dolls, and later for her mother's various charitable guilds. The rest of her day was set aside for outdoor activities, usually riding on her own, or cycling with her brothers, and sometimes an improvised game of cricket under the watchful eye of Hansell. She also enjoyed lawn tennis, angling and swimming.

At the age of six she was given her first donkey, called Ben, on whom she doted. The others saw that she had the makings of a first-class horsewoman, and Albert later remarked that 'My sister was a horse until she came out'. Edward admiringly commented that 'her yellow curls concealed a fearlessness that commanded our respect'.[14] She eagerly devoured the boys' adventure stories of R.M. Ballantyne, H. Rider Haggard and Robert Louis Stevenson, and shared most of her brothers' activities. This did not stop her from 'wielding a sweet tyranny' over her brothers' lives, with Mademoiselle ever in support.

Though in awe of her gruff father, she found him less intimidating than her brothers did, and he was not so strict with her. She grew up very like her mother in personality, and inherited her low-pitched voice. Musically talented, she took singing lessons at Frogmore, while her brothers lurked beneath the music-room window, making noises imitating the midnight serenades of a lovesick tomcat. She also became an accomplished pianist, though her father's indulgence did not extend to her regularly playing scales within earshot. She therefore had to use the piano at the 'big house', Sandringham, where her increasingly deaf grandmother was not disturbed at all. As a young woman Queen Alexandra had enjoyed music herself, and she would have been the last to discourage such talent in her grandchildren.

Like her brothers, Mary led a very isolated childhood. For perhaps weeks at a time, she saw no other girls at all; the only women with whom she came into contact were her tutors and female members of her staff. Else was her closest friend and personal confidante, and she would talk to her as a sister. Even so, there were doubtless times when she missed having no female companions of her own age.

As the two elder boys approached their teens, Edward was becoming too old for such confined educational instruction, and Albert began to resent his elder brother's superiority. The presence of one, Hansell thought, was acting as 'a sort of "red rag" to the other'.

Edward had been destined from birth for the Royal Navy. The only condition enjoined on his tutors by his father was that the boy should be taught enough to be able to pass the entrance examination. Latin and Greek were not required at sea, therefore the Prince of Wales saw no point in his learning them. Neither did Mr Hansell have any illusions as to the shortcomings of his tutoring under such tightly controlled conditions. If he was ever to be able to hold his own with his contemporaries, Hansell warned, the Prince ought to go to a good preparatory school. 'What I suspect he most feared for me was that, in consequence of my being deprived of the communal habits of thought and behaviour that are absorbed at an early age in a private school,' wrote the Prince, 'I was bound at first to feel lonely and insecure when brought into close association with my contemporaries.' Such theories carried no weight with the Prince of Wales. Neither he nor his brother had ever been to a preparatory school; 'the Navy will teach David all that he needs to know'.[15]

In spring 1907 Edward was enrolled as a cadet at the Royal Naval College, Osborne. Henry, now aged seven, joined the schoolroom, and Albert was grandly promoted to the 'position' of head boy.

It had been decided that he, too, would go to Osborne in due course. He was weak at and hated mathematics, but thanks to his tutor Martin David, and supreme persistence on his part, he made sufficient progress in the subject to face the Examining Board in November 1908. The six members of the board agreed afterwards that he was the most shy and nervous candidate to come before them, but he showed his capacity of rising to the occasion, which was to stand him in good stead many years hence. Though he began by stammering badly, he mastered his nerves and answered the questions 'brightly and well'. Had he been a costermonger's son, one of them remarked, there would not have been the slightest hesitation in passing him. He took the written entrance examination in December, and achieved good marks in English, history and French.

The intentions of the authorities to treat the Princes much as they would the other boys were difficult to put into practice. The end of the summer term 1909 was enlivened by preparations for a state visit by Tsar Nicholas II and his family, who were to arrive at

Spithead in the imperial yacht on 2 August. Edward, Albert and Mary were to act as companions for the Grand Duchesses and the Tsarevich Alexis. While staying with his parents at Barton Manor, Albert caught a cold, subsequently developed whooping-cough, and had to be kept in quarantine until after the imperial guests had departed. The risk to the haemophiliac Tsarevich Alexis of catching the infection and rupturing a blood vessel from prolonged bouts of coughing was too great, and it was left to Edward to show his uncle around Osborne, while Mary was to be a playmate for the Grand Duchesses.

Though the young generation of Romanovs spent less than a day on British soil, they remembered it for the rest of their unhappy lives. Life at home, at Tsarskoe-Selo, near St Petersburg, was a gloomy business. The four Grand Duchesses, aged between thirteen and seven at the time of the Osborne visit, led an oddly isolated existence. They were not allowed female companions, as the Tsarina dreaded them having the companionship of 'over-sophisticated young women of the aristocracy' brought up on a diet of gossip in an apparently decadent society. The girls adored each other and never quarrelled among themselves. This could be taken for lack of personality; it more probably resulted from the perpetual anxiety which overshadowed their lives and those of their parents. Their tutor, Pierre Gilliard, was intrigued to see the Tsarevich dropping in on their lessons from time to time, then disappearing for days at a time. Everyone, he noticed, would be smitten with the deepest depression, and his sisters would only tell him cryptically that he 'was not well'. Not for years did Gilliard find out the real reason. The Tsarina's health was shattered by the strain of watching her son suffer, and the Tsar was perpetually 'completely run down mentally', in his own words, by worry over her health, in addition to his other problems.

At Osborne, briefly away from such anxieties, and able to see once more the island home where she had shared holidays with her mother as a small girl, and later been taken under the protective wing of her grandmother, the Tsarina was almost a different person. When not being shown round Osborne, the Grand Duchesses played on the beach, looking for seashells, buying postcards and rock, which they eagerly offered later to their parents.

Meanwhile Prince Louis Francis of Battenberg, or 'Dickie', was enjoying a rather more relaxed childhood than his peers. Eight years younger than his brother George, at the time of his birth his sisters were aged fifteen and eleven respectively. With this difference in ages, he grew up a rather solitary child. According to his aunt Princess Anna, when the Battenberg children came to tea, George and their sister Louise sat sedately at table, while Dickie settled in a corner, conducting an animated conversation with an invisible friend.

Left to entertain himself, he developed an imaginative streak. One day his Uncle Ernie, Grand Duke of Hesse, saw him drawing a picture of a cow with an extraordinary head and five legs. When he pointed out that this was hardly a lifelike cow, Dickie said indignantly that it was not a cow, it was a 'Katuf'. The name was henceforth adopted for family use to describe any sort of fanciful animal. He loved reading, especially the novels of Edith Nesbit, and works of fantasy such as *Alice in Wonderland* and *Through the Looking-Glass*, and *The Wizard of Oz*.

His father was often away on active service, and he spent much of his time with his mother, accompanying her on many of her journeys. As the child of a naval officer, it was inevitable that travel would be a major part of his life; as one who had cousins in Germany and Russia, he enjoyed many holidays abroad as a small child. At Wolfsgarten, the country retreat of Uncle Ernie, was a miniature playhouse that he and the Grand Duchess had built for their daughter Elizabeth.* All the young cousins who came to stay enjoyed a rough-and-tumble within its walls. Even if they could crouch down and make themselves small enough, adults were expressly forbidden to enter the little house. Many a royal nurse or tutor would pace up and down impatiently outside, waiting for their high-spirited young charges to stop their games out of sheer exhaustion and emerge for more mundane tasks.

The Grand Duke of Hesse was keenly interested in aviation, and

---

*The Grand Duke of Hesse had married his cousin Princess Victoria Melita of Edinburgh in 1894, but their relationship was stormy, and they divorced in 1901. Elizabeth, their only child, died of typhoid in November 1903, aged eight.

provided Dickie with his first experience of flying. In 1906 he arranged for an airship to come to his country seat, Wolfsgarten, and take the family for a ride. At six, Dickie was considered too young to fly, but at the last moment more ballast was needed; Uncle Ernie reached out of the gondola and, much to his delight, dragged Dickie aboard by his collar.

With its rapid advances in scientific discovery and technological change, the first decade of the twentieth century was an exciting time for any child fascinated by new inventions and gadgets. He was only three when his father told them that he had bought a car; they were the first of any branch of their family, he proudly recalled, to own one. Two years later, he was allowed to record his voice on a wax cylinder and hear it played back through a phonograph. The experience thrilled him, even if he was probably unable to recognize his own voice in the distorted sound.

Pets played an important part in his childhood. One of his earliest memories was being given a canary for his third birthday. It was so tame that it was allowed to be left outside its cage. Unhappily he tried to pick it up, lost his balance, and ended up crushing it. Later on there was Scamp, a black rough haired mongrel, a procession of white rabbits, and on his seventh birthday a lamb named Millie. As she was not always obedient, he put a running noose around her neck, so she would choke if she refused to follow him. When told that this was unkind, he tied the cord to one her legs instead. She followed him under protest, still making choking noises.

In January 1905 he went to school for the first time, attending classes at Macpherson's Gymnasium. At the end of each class the boys would assemble for a patriotic sing-song. Not being wholly confident of the words, he would sing, 'Rue Britannia, Britannia rue the waves!' Four years later he attended a more formal establishment, Mr Gladstone's School, Cliveden Place. In his first termly order he came bottom of the class in arithmetic. Never very academic, in most other subjects he came about two-thirds of the way down the class. Yet the teachers gave him credit for his excellent conduct and persistent efforts to improve his performance.

9

'The securest and happiest lot humankind had ever known'

As a third son, Prince Henry was fortunate enough to escape the pressures to which his elder brothers were subjected. There was little chance of him ascending the throne, and persistent ill-health in infancy gave him some advantage. Sickly and undersized (although he grew up to be taller than his brothers), he suffered from weakness in the legs as well as knock-knees, and perpetual colds. After a bout of influenza in February 1909, Hansell was reprimanded by his father for having taken him out that week in the bitter cold at Sandringham; the tutor must 'remember that he is rather fragile & must be treated differently to his two elder brothers who are more robust'.[1]

Like them, he was to go to Royal Naval College, remaining in Hansell's schoolroom at York Cottage until the age of twelve or so. However, influenza affected the base of one lung, and it was decided that he would be unable to face the rigours of college. Dr Laking offered his premises at Broadstairs as a suitable place for the boy to convalesce, and he was sent there with the Prince of Wales's nurse, Sister Edith Ward, to look after him and continue his education.

They arrived there in February 1910. As part of his education, Henry wrote to his parents regularly, and kept a daily diary as a spelling and writing exercise. He dutifully recorded such activities as the pleasures of the sands, fossil and shell hunting, the electric tram to Ramsgate, walks on the eastern esplanade and the pier at Margate, and French lessons taken by Mlle de Lisle, from Folkestone. On his fossil hunts he was accompanied by Mr A.J. Richardson, headmaster of St Peter's Court, and a friend of Hansell. The latter had already been in touch with him, with a view to enrolling the

Prince at his school. Having failed to persuade the Prince and Princess of Wales to send the two elder boys to school, he hoped to convince them that the third might go instead. The father's letters to his son were full of admonitions that he must behave like a boy and not like a little child, and Hansell recognized that this was more likely to be achieved if the boy went to school instead of remaining under the care of a nurse. On 2 May 1910 Richardson was invited to Marlborough House by Hansell for a long talk. Sister Edith had agreed that the boy should be given a 'careful trial' of school life as a day pupil, while continuing to live under her supervision at York Gate House.

That same week, the Prince of Wales's two eldest sons were at Marlborough House, preparing to return to Osborne and Dartmouth for the summer term. On 5 May, the day before they were due to go back, their father sent for them. Anxiously, he warned them that 'Grandpapa' was very ill, 'and the end may not be far off'.[2]

Two days later Edward was woken in the morning by a cry from his brother Bertie, who had looked out of the window and seen the standard at half-mast. 'Across the Mall, Buckingham Palace stood grey and silent.'[3] King Edward VII had died, aged sixty-eight. Although he had a long history of bronchial trouble, neither the family nor the British public had realized quite how suddenly the end had come. Queen Alexandra and her unmarried daughter Victoria had been summoned back from a Mediterranean holiday on 5 May, and sat with the King at Buckingham Palace until he drew his last breath a few minutes before midnight the following day.

Henry's response was uncomplicated and sincere. 'I am so awfuly [sic] sorry that dear Grandpapa is dead, and that you, Mama, Grannie and Aunt Toria are in such trouble,' he wrote to his father, now King George V, from York Gate House (8 May). 'I shall try to help you by being a good boy.'[4]

Soon after being told of his grandfather's death, four-year-old John made a pile of leaves in the garden. He had been told that the spirits of dead people leave their bodies to inhabit the wind, and when asked what he was doing, he replied mournfully, 'sweeping up Grandpa's bits'.[5]

Various poetic euphemisms were used to try to cushion younger royal children from the full horrors of death. Alice of Albany, who had married Queen Mary's youngest brother Alexander, was visiting her brother Charles, now Duke of Saxe-Coburg Gotha. With them went their three children. The youngest, Maurice, aged less than six months, died in September, a tragedy ascribed by his mother to a change from English to German diet. His sister Mary, then aged four, was puzzled when one day he was not to be seen anywhere, and all the family around her wore the deepest black without explaining to her what had happened. A room to which she had previously been admitted was locked, and she was forbidden to go near. Only the day after his funeral was she taken to his tiny grave and told that Maurice had 'gone to the angels'.[6]

For Prince Edward in particular, the death of his grandfather meant considerable changes. He automatically became Duke of Cornwall, inheriting large estates in the West Country and at Kennington in London. Heir to the throne, he was created Prince of Wales on his birthday on 23 June, six weeks later. His childhood was over. The next day, he was confirmed by Dr Randall Davidson, Archbishop of Canterbury, in the private chapel of Windsor Castle.

Though his childhood was over, his formal education was not. He had gone back to Dartmouth after King Edward VII's funeral on 20 May, having missed three weeks of the summer term. The other cadets, he noted, welcomed him back 'with appropriate condolences', but he could not help noticing a subtle, even fawning, respect for his new position. While the cadets continued to call him Prince Edward, on parade and in the classroom he was Duke of Cornwall and Heir Apparent. Later that year, while convalescing at Newquay from mumps and measles, the King told him that he would have to leave Dartmouth, in order to play a prominent role in the Coronation in June 1911.

That summer the King and his family headed north for Balmoral. One of their guests that September was David Lloyd George, Chancellor of the Exchequer. Lloyd George was no respecter of the institution of monarchy, and for much of his career regarded King George V with less than total tolerance, but he left a surprisingly relaxed portrayal of the family at lunch one day. Though the King was something of a tyrant to his children, in front of a senior minister he was careful to give a better impression. After lunch when the cigars were brought around,

Lloyd George recalled, the Queen stayed to smoke a cigarette, and the boys began to blow out the cigar lights as a game. Mary wanted to join in and got very excited, 'then the Queen and the rest of us joined in and the noise was deafening until the little Princess set her lamp on fire. We thought then it was time to stop.'[7]

The other Princes were still being educated. 'Cadet Prince Albert' was also due to go from Osborne to Dartmouth in due course, if he could achieve the right academic grade. Like his father and grandfather, he was not a natural student. At the end of each term he was rarely far from bottom of his class. Nevertheless, he joined Edward (in his final term) at Dartmouth in January 1911.

Henry became the first son of a British monarch to go to school. After his first three days as a day boy at St Peters Court, he told his father that he liked it, and on Hansell's advice he was enrolled as an ordinary boarder, so that he would be subject to proper discipline like any other boy of his age. Naturally it turned out not to be quite as simple as that; for the school authorities and the other boys, it was quite a novelty to have a Prince in their midst. They did not know how to address him; 'Prince Henry' seemed rather cumbersome, Christian names were not then in common usage at prep schools, and although the reigning house was then the house of Saxe-Coburg Gotha, it was debatable as to whether members of the royal family should use that as a surname.

His academic progress was slow, but he had started late in the term. He had also pleased his father and tutor by his good behaviour; their greatest fear had been that he would lose his temper if provoked by the other boys, but this was never to be a problem. Academically he was not very bright, though unlike his elder brothers he was good at mathematics. There was an outbreak of mumps at school in the spring, but though Henry was confined to bed in the third week of May, he recovered in time for the Coronation on 22 June.

All the younger children, except John, sat watching from the royal gallery in Westminster Abbey. John was considered too young and too mischievous to sit through the ceremony, but he was allowed to watch the processions from a window in the state apartments of Buckingham Palace. (Edward, wearing the robes of the Order of the Garter, had taken his place below with the other peers of the realm). Albert was in naval dress uniform, Mary in a robe of state, Henry and George in Highland dress. On their way to the Abbey, riding in a coach in the Prince of Wales's procession, they behaved impeccably. On the way back they became bored. The two youngest boys had a fight in full view of the amused spectators, and in trying to stop them Mary's coronet was almost knocked off.

One of the children's playmates was their cousin Crown Prince Olav of Norway, son of King George's youngest sister Maud, who had married Prince Charles of Denmark in 1896. Though she had never harboured regal aspirations on her marriage, in 1905 Norway proclaimed its independence from Sweden, her husband was elected King, taking the title of Haakon VII, and with some reluctance she found herself Queen Consort. Her only child was born in July 1903 at Appleton, Sandringham.* He was a ready playmate for his cousins, and the four of them would join in games at Sandringham with miniature forts, cannon and lead soldiers.

King George V took a keen interest in these games, but imposed one rule of his own: the 'armies' were not to be named after any existing countries, so the battles had to be between different planets, such as Earth and Mars. The boys also dressed up in cocked hats, made wooden swords, and drilled each other. After visiting a military tournament, George introduced some variations of his own and made them 'break step' when crossing a bridge. Afterwards he explained that this was in case the masonry should become dislodged by the rhythm of their marching feet. At other times they played cowboys and Indians, a traditional version with Buffalo Bill as the hero.

The English royal family's children were allowed to play with their toys and indulge in games lightheartedly enough, a privilege denied their German cousins. When the court photographer Richard Speaight visited Berlin in 1908 to take photographs of the Crown Princess and her two samll sons, he took with him a collection of mechanical toys to amuse them. Though they

---

*He was initially called Alexander, but given the more Norwegian name of Olav when his parents became King and Queen.

understood English, they were not interested in such objects. Keen to elicit some response from the children, he crawled on the floor on all fours and threw a rug over his back, pretending to be an elephant. They continued to stare at him, stony-faced and silent. Taking pity on him, the Crown Princess told him that he would never get her boys to obey him until he treated them as soldiers. As they were being brought up in an entirely military environment, they only thought in terms of drilling and war.[8]

In the summer term of 1912 George accompanied Henry on his return to St Peter's Court. George was the least shy of the brothers, also the most talented and intellectually gifted. Academically, musically and culturally he outshone them all. Nearly three years younger than Henry, he quickly rivalled the elder boy's performance.

Henry's progress at schoolwork was pedestrian, particularly at classics. Mathematics still proved his best subject, and he came top of the form in the first term. He preferred sports and became an enthusiastic cricketer, taking three wickets and scoring sixty runs not out in one match. The King was unimpressed: 'the bowling couldn't have been very famous'. His soccer and squash rackets found more favour with his father, both being 'capital games'. This time it was the Queen's turn to complain (2 November 1912): 'Do for goodness sake wake up and work harder and use the brains God has given you. All you write about is your everlasting football of which I am heartily sick.'[9]

Henry finished at St Peter's Court at the end of the summer term 1913, and in the autumn term started at Eton, where he was put in the same house as Prince Leopold, later King of the Belgians. Apart from being met by a royal brougham at Slough on arriving for his first day, he was treated with very little privilege. One minor modification was made to his curriculum. The King asked that he should not be taught Latin, but French and German instead, as both modern languages would be far more practical value to a prince of the royal house than a classical one. He never ceased to rue the deficiencies in his own lamentable linguistic education.

Henry's masters wrote on his reports that he was 'thoroughly cheerful modest & obedient', throwing himself into the life of the school very willingly. Several other boys asked for photographs of him, as they had done of his elder brothers at college. They had been given unlimited supplies of prints, but he was not similarly favoured. The Queen told him to order some more, warning him that they cost one shilling each.

Even at Eton, he was aware of the unsettling times in which they lived. Queen Mary had written to him describing how she had seen the police arresting suffragettes trying to get past the gates at Buckingham Palace. Information came from Scotland Yard that a suffragette plan was being hatched in Liverpool to 'molest' Henry at Eton, and a policeman was posted to keep a discreet eye on him at school just in case. The Ulster Home Rule crisis, which dominated domestic politics early in 1914, so distracted the King that he was too busy to write his usual birthday letter to Henry in March, so the Queen sent his good wishes with hers. In addition there was some difficulty, albeit less so than in a later age, of protecting the Prince from journalists and photographers. At least one October afternoon on the games field was spoilt, he wrote, by 'a beastly photographer . . . trying to take photos of me playing footer which would not have been much of a sight'.[10]

Prince John was now left alone in the nursery and schoolroom, a source of great anxiety to parents and nurse. Mrs Bill disliked him living at the palace, particularly as the gardens were so large that he would play dangerous tricks with his bicycle when out of sight. Moreover, the fits were becoming more frequent and more severe, and the doctors warned that he would not live to adulthood. He was given a basic education; he could read, and wrote well, but his parents and tutors decided that it would be only kind to tax him as little as possible during the few years left. He was kept increasingly isolated from his brothers and sister, as they found the attacks so distressing. At the back of the adults' minds was a fear that he could easily have a fatal fit in front of his family.

The widowed Queen Alexandra was particularly fond of him. She had always been attached to her children when they were young, and increasing deafness had cut her off more and more from people other than family and long-standing friends. In her own childlike, unsophisticated way, she seemed more hopeful that the boy might be cured than his more down-to-earth parents ever were. Yet the fact that he seemed unlikely to grow up gave her comfort, as she could 'baby' him to her heart's content without being reproached.

Most of her widowhood was spent at Sandringham, and she often asked for the 'precious and dear little boy' to join her for tea, games, jigsaw puzzles, or listen to music together. Grandmother and grandchild were a great mutual comfort.*

In May 1910, the first month of the new reign, Dickie Battenberg was driven to Locker's Park School near Berkhamsted, Hertfordshire. The other boys were not particularly impressed by the fact that he was a Serene Highness. At first he was homesick and missed his family and pets, but he persevered, and two years later he was top of his class in Latin and English. Encouraged never to forget his royal origins yet not boast about them, he was warned not to get so excited about going to Windsor for the funeral of King Edward VII in May 1910 that he neglected his work. He was anxious to attend the Coronation the following year, not least as it would mean missing a few lessons, but was told he was too young to attend the ceremony and had to be content with an invitation to Buckingham Palace where he could watch the King and Queen leaving in the gold coach. In May 1913, six weeks before his thirteenth birthday, he followed his cousins and entered the Royal Naval College at Osborne.

How much the younger royal children were aware of the gathering storms throughout Europe in the summer of 1914 is a matter for conjecture. Henry knew from his mother's letters that there were grave crises looming, although matters seemed less serious on the Continent than at home. The King and Queen could barely appear in public – particularly at the races, or the theatre – without a suffragette demonstration. The rejection of the Irish Home Rule bill in the House of Lords made civil war between Catholics and Protestants likely, and the situation in Europe looked ever more uneasy after the assassination of the Austrian heir, Archduke Francis Ferdinand and his wife, at Sarajevo on 28 June 1914. 'I was so sad about the assassination of the Austrian heir,'[11] Henry wrote dutifully (5 July 1914).

*In 1917, when Prince John was twelve, the decision was taken to isolate him. He and Mrs Bill lived at Wood Farm on the Sandringham estate, where in January 1919 he had a particularly bad seizure and died peacefully in his sleep.

To some, including the King and most of his ministers, it was a 'terrible shock for the dear old Emperor', Francis Joseph, and another deeply regrettable anarchist outrage but perhaps no more. Others saw it differently. On the following morning Fraülein Kuebler, German governess to the children of the Earl of Strathmore, came down to breakfast at their London house, St James's Square, to be met by a sea of gloomy faces at the table. Lord Strathmore thrust a copy of the *Morning Post* at her, with its front page news about the assassinations. 'This means war!' he exclaimed. Even so, when the governess went on holiday two weeks later to visit her German home for her parents' silver wedding, Lady Strathmore embraced her emotionally, begging her to promise that she would be back.

Many other governesses in England faced the same dilemma. At Buckingham Palace, Princess Mary's devoted maid, Else Korsukawitz, also looked at the news with mounting concern.*

Prince Louis could not fail to appreciate that his father, as First Sea Lord, was increasingly preoccupied with ensuring the naval state of readiness, should the worst come to the worst. By the end of July the situation looked bleak.

On 4 August Lady Elizabeth Lyon, youngest daughter of the Earl of Strathmore, celebrated her fourteenth birthday. As a treat that evening, her mother had booked a box at the Coliseum in the West End to see a variety show. Their journey to the theatre by car was reduced to a crawl by crowds mad with excitement, frantically cheering as they waved Union Jacks. Every topical reference to events delivered on stage was received with cheering and prolonged clapping. The minutes were slowly ticking away, as Great Britain'a ultimatum to Germany came closer to expiry. No answer was received, and many a child within earshot of Buckingham Palace at midnight heard the hysterical enthusiasm of the crowds as the chimes of midnight struck. Great Britain was at war with Germany.

---

*Else Korsukawitz left royal service a few weeks after the outbreak of war. She was as reluctant to return to Germany as the King and Queen were to see her go, but if she stayed with them she would have risked internment as an enemy alien.

Between the birth of Princess Victoria of Kent at Kensington Palace, and the outbreak of war between Britain and Germany ninety-five years later, the world had changed beyond recognition. At the age of seventeen, the Princess had been captivated by her first sight of a railway train; some eighty years later, her small great-grandsons thought it the height of adventure to be riding at thirty miles per hour in a car, or travelling in an aeroplane. The future Queen had played with dolls and mechanical toys; her descendants would grow up with the motion picture and the phonograph.

The world, wrote French poet Charles Péguy in 1913, had changed less since Jesus Christ than it had in the last thirty years.[12] In the words of historian Arthur Bryant some twenty years later, it was the age of great parks with their noble trees, slumbering in the sunlight of distant summers, while 'children born heirs to the securest and happiest lot humankind had ever known, rode and played in their shade never guessing that in their old age they would see the classic groves felled by the estate breaker and the stately halls pulled down or sold to make convalescent homes for miners or county asylums'.[13]

Such was not the fate of royal children born in the Victorian era, though most of them who lived to middle age or more would become increasingly perplexed at the changes wrought on their country by the twentieth century. They had been brought up in what Meriel Buchanan, daughter of a former Ambassador to the court of St Petersburg and the friend of many a prince or princess, fondly described as the England of 'sleepy little villages, with no strident discord of the radio or of television echoing out of the windows, no chain-stores to oust the quaint little shops kept by elderly ladies'.[14]

Throughout these years, childhood at court had been very different for most of its illustrious personages. From Princess Victoria, who grew up an only child, almost completely in isolation from her peers; from her closely knit nine children, some of whom grew up under the shadow of Baron Stockmar and a succession of tutors; to the children of the Prince of Wales, 'undisciplined, wild as hawks', and the children of his son, 'a regiment, not a family'. It was a life of privilege, but not untrammelled luxury; a life of duty and responsibility towards others. Life, the Prince Consort had warned his eldest son on the latter's seventeenth birthday, was 'composed of duties'. One might almost imagine the saying, embroidered on a needlework sampler, framed and hung up above every royal child's bed.

'One hates parting, even from an imaginary bit of a past so precious, and one loves not beginning a new phase and embarking on the unknown.'[15] The Empress Frederick wrote these words on the first day of the twentieth century, but although she was referring to the century just gone, she might equally have been referring to her happy childhood. While her mother had known loneliness, and while some – thankfully only a very few – from succeeding generations had endured misery or torture at the hands of unsympathetic tutors or nurses, for most of the children at court in the nineteenth century, childhood had indeed been the happiest days of their lives.

THE ANCESTRY AND IMMEDIATE DESCENDANTS OF
QUEEN VICTORIA AND PRINCE ALBERT

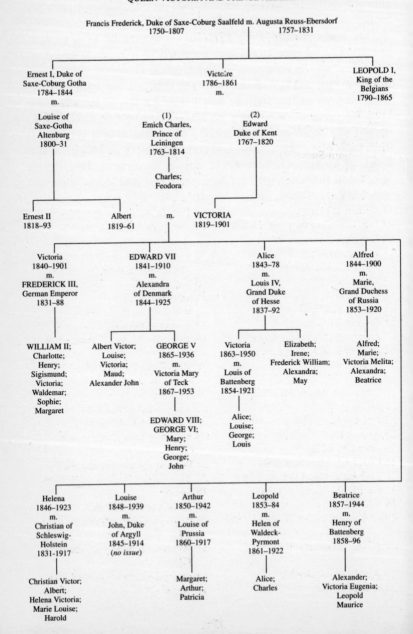

Francis Frederick, Duke of Saxe-Coburg Saalfeld m. Augusta Reuss-Ebersdorf
1750–1807   1757–1831

Ernest I, Duke of
Saxe-Coburg Gotha
1784–1844
m.

Victoire
1786–1861
m.

LEOPOLD I,
King of the
Belgians
1790–1865

Louise of
Saxe-Gotha
Altenburg
1800–31

(1)
Emich Charles,
Prince of
Leiningen
1763–1814

(2)
Edward
Duke of Kent
1767–1820

Charles;
Feodora

Ernest II
1818–93

Albert
1819–61

m.

VICTORIA
1819–1901

Victoria
1840–1901
m.
FREDERICK III,
German Emperor
1831–88

EDWARD VII
1841–1910
m.
Alexandra
of Denmark
1844–1925

Alice
1843–78
m.
Louis IV,
Grand Duke
of Hesse
1837–92

Alfred
1844–1900
m.
Marie,
Grand Duchess
of Russia
1853–1920

WILLIAM II;
Charlotte;
Henry;
Sigismund;
Victoria;
Waldemar;
Sophie;
Margaret

Albert Victor;
Louise;
Victoria;
Maud;
Alexander John

GEORGE V
1865–1936
m.
Victoria Mary
of Teck
1867–1953

Victoria
1863–1950
m.
Louis of
Battenberg
1854–1921

Elizabeth;
Irene;
Frederick William;
Alexandra;
May

Alfred;
Marie;
Victoria Melita;
Alexandra;
Beatrice

EDWARD VIII;
GEORGE VI;
Mary;
Henry;
George;
John

Alice;
Louise;
George;
Louis

Helena
1846–1923
m.
Christian of
Schleswig-
Holstein
1831–1917

Louise
1848–1939
m.
John, Duke
of Argyll
1845–1914
(no issue)

Arthur
1850–1942
m.
Louise of
Prussia
1860–1917

Leopold
1853–84
m.
Helen of
Waldeck-
Pyrmont
1861–1922

Beatrice
1857–1944
m.
Henry of
Battenberg
1858–96

Christian Victor;
Albert;
Helena Victoria;
Marie Louise;
Harold

Margaret;
Arthur;
Patricia

Alice;
Charles

Alexander;
Victoria Eugenia;
Leopold
Maurice

Reference Notes

CHAPTER 1 *(pp. 1–25)*

1 *Letters of Queen Victoria* I i 18
2 Marie of Roumania I 4
3 Hughes 3
4 Woodham-Smith 30
5 ibid 34
6 ibid 41
7 ibid 47
8 Mullen & Munson 7
9 *Letters of Queen Victoria* I i 11
10 Longford, *Victoria R.I.* 22
11 Woodham-Smith 74–5
12 Mullen & Munson 7
13 Weintraub 57
14 Mullen & Munson 7
15 Keppel, G.T. 310
16 *Dearest Child* 111–2
17 *Letters of Queen Victoria* I i 18
18 Longford, *Victoria R.I.* 32;
   Woodham-Smith 76
19 Charlot 51
20 *Girlhood of Queen Victoria* I 16
21 ibid 43
22 ibid 44–5
23 ibid 124
24 Greville I 412
25 Longford, *Victoria R.I.* 44
26 *Girlhood of Queen Victoria* I 181
27 Longford, *Victoria R.I.* 54
28 ibid 57
29 *Girlhood of Queen Victoria* I 196

CHAPTER 2 *(pp. 26–50)*

1 Woodham-Smith 217
2 Martin I 100

3 ibid 101
4 Longford, *Victoria R.I.* 154
5 Bennett, *Queen Victoria's children* 33
6 *Letters of Queen Victoria* I i 255
7 ibid
8 Hibbert 115
9 Woodham-Smith 224
10 Magnus 1
11 Longford, *Victoria R.I.* 159
12 *Letters of Queen Victoria* I i 364–5
13 ibid 364
14 Longford, *Victoria R.I.* 160
15 ibid
16 Lyttelton 327
17 ibid 332
18 Woodham-Smith 233
19 *The Empress Frederick writes to Sophie* 199–200
20 Woodham-Smith 268
21 Lyttelton 339
22 ibid 340
23 Longford, *Victoria R.I.* 174
24 Bolitho, *Prince Consort* 72
25 *Letters of the Prince Consort* 103–4
26 Bolitho, *Prince Consort* 86–7
27 *Alice, Grand Duchess of Hesse* 6
28 ibid 8
29 Woodham-Smith 267
30 Bennett, *Queen Victoria's children* 28
31 Weintraub, *Importance of being Edward* 7
32 *Letters of Queen Victoria* I i 365
33 Magnus 4

34 Bennett, *Queen Victoria's children* 56–7
35 Woodham-Smith 266
36 ibid 268
37 ibid 368–9
38 ibid 383
39 Pakula 42
38 Belton 159

CHAPTER 3 (pp. 51–75)

1 Lyttelton 383
2 ibid 409–10
3 Woodham-Smith 335–6
4 Lee I 29–30
5 Magnus 7–8
6 ibid 8
7 Longford, *Victoria R.I.* 218
8 Magnus 9
9 ibid 14
10 Van der Kiste & Jordaan 20
11 ibid 20–1
12 *Further letters of Queen Victoria* 75
13 Greville VII 388–9
14 Nicolson 14
15 Stanley 38
16 Journal of Prince Alfred, July 1852
17 Rowell 82
18 ibid 84
19 Epton 59
20 Ormond & Blackett-Ord 195
21 *Dearest Mama* 116
22 Stanley 46
23 'This brilliant year' 30
24 *Illustrated London News*, 31 March 1855
25 Martin III 240
26 Van der Kiste & Jordaan 24
27 Victoria, Queen, *Leaves* 153
28 Victoria, Queen, *Further letters* 62
29 ibid 63–4

30 Jim Hanson Letters
31 *Letters of the Prince Consort* 272–3

CHAPTER 4 (pp. 76–89)

1 Stanley 146
2 ibid 206
3 Duff, *Hessian tapestry* 270
4 Priestley 20
5 Aston 49
6 McClintock 26
7 ibid 25
8 ibid 28
9 St Aubyn, *Edward VII* 24
10 Magnus 18
11 ibid 22
12 ibid 22
13 Esher 10
14 Martin IV 30
15 *Dearest Child* 28
16 Magnus 26
17 *Dearest Child* 144
18 ibid 134
19 ibid 141
20 Epton 92
21 Stanley 246
22 *Daily Telegraph*, 24 December 1861
23 Thurston Letters
24 *Dearest Mama* 198
25 Aston 51

CHAPTER 5 (pp. 90–102)

1 Stanley 283
2 Frith I 351–3
3 McClintock 52
4 ibid 54
5 ibid 55
6 ibid 55
7 ibid 56
8 Bryant 12
9 McClintock 56

10 *Dearest Mama* 312
11 Battiscombe 65
12 Jim Hanson Letters
13 Gore 13–4
14 Battiscombe 122–3
15 *Your dear letter* 222
16 ibid 122
17 Gore 24
18 Nicolson 7–8

CHAPTER 6 (*pp. 103–29*)

1 Jim Hanson Letters
2 Warren 7
3 Longford, *Victoria R.I.* 386
4 Marie of Roumania I 40
5 *Beloved Mama* 87
6 Nicolson, *George V* 12–3
7 ibid 14
8 Gore 31–2
9 Marie of Roumania I 53
10 ibid 12
11 ibid 4
12 ibid 12
13 ibid 14
14 ibid 59
15 Millais 292–3
16 Marie of Roumania I 173
17 ibid 30
18 Battiscombe 142–3
19 St Aubyn, *Edward VII* 103
20 Battiscombe 143
21 Warren 20
22 ibid 30
23 ibid 43
24 Argyll Etkin Ltd Letters
25 Warren 61
26 ibid 66
27 Alice, *For my grandchildren* 52
28 Argyll Etkin Ltd Letters
29 Alice 63
30 ibid 68
31 ibid 70

CHAPTER 7 (*pp. 130–45*)

1 Jim Hanson Letters
2 Duff, *Hessian tapestry* 270
3 Hough, *Advice* 3
4 ibid 267
5 Mallet 57–8
6 Duff, *Hessian tapestry* 188
7 Pimlott 4
8 Dalton 16
9 ibid 15
10 Pimlott 421
11 Noel, *Ena* 14
12 ibid 13
13 Hibbert 417
14 Nicolson, *Diaries* 359
15 Jim Hanson Letters
16 Epton 224
17 *Royalty Digest* I 98
18 *Beloved and darling child* 68
19 Windsor, Duke of, *Family album* 23
20 ibid 21
21 Gore 180
22 Wheeler-Bennett 181
23 Windsor, Duke of, *King's story* 24
24 Pope-Hennessy 392
25 Windsor, Duke of, *King's story* 25
26 ibid 27
27 Longford, *Royal house of Windsor* 45
28 Windsor, Duke of, *King's story* 13
29 Van der Kiste, *Princess Victoria Melita* 73

CHAPTER 8 (*pp. 146–62*)

1 Windsor, Duke of, *King's story* 14–15
2 Pope-Hennessy 394–5
3 Keppel, Sonia 23

4 Windsor, Duke of, *King's story*
19
5 ibid 22
6 Wheeler-Bennett 25
7 Windsor, Duke of, *King's story*
29
8 Windsor, Duke of, *Family album*
24
9 ibid
10 Noel, *Ena* 8
11 Alice, *For my grandchildren* 78
12 Wheeler-Bennett 28
13 Carey 29
14 Windsor, Duke of, *King's story*
42
15 ibid 57

CHAPTER 9 *(pp. 163–73)*

1 Frankland 11
2 Windsor, Duke of, *King's story* 68
3 ibid 69
4 Frankland 15
5 *Royalty Digest* II 73
6 ibid IV 11
7 Morgan 53
8 Speaight 80
9 Frankland 27
10 ibid 31
11 ibid 35
12 Shattuck 1
13 Bryant 233
14 Buchanan 1
15 *Letters of the Empress Frederick*
464

Bibliography

I UNPUBLISHED MANUSCRIPTS

Argyll Etkin Ltd Letters
Jim Hanson Letters
Letters from Mary Ann Thurston (in private possession)
Prince Alfred's journal, 1851–5 (Bayerisches Staatsarchiv, Coburg)

II BOOKS

Albert, Prince Consort, *Letters of the Prince Consort, 1831–1861;* (ed.)
Kurt Jagow. John Murray, 1938
Alice, Grand Duchess of Hesse, *Princess of Great Britain and Ireland:
biographical sketch and letters.* John Murray, 1884
Alice, Princess, Countess of Athlone, *For my grandchildren: some
reminiscences.* Evans Bros, 1966
Aston, Sir George, *His Royal Highness the Duke of Connaught and
Strathearn: a life and intimate study.* Harrap, 1929
Baird, Diana (arr.), *Victorian days and a Royal Friendship.* Littlebury, 1958
[Comprises, in part, correspondence between Princess Christian and
Emily Baird]
Battiscombe, Georgina, *Queen Alexandra.* Constable, 1969
Belton, Fred, *Random recollections of an old actor.* Tinsley, 1880
Bennett, Daphne, *King without a crown: Albert, Prince Consort of England
1819–1861.* Heinemann, 1977
—— *Queen Victoria's children.* Victor Gollancz, 1980
—— *Vicky, Princess Royal of England and German Empress.* Collins Harvill,
1971
Bolitho, Hector (ed.), *The Prince Consort and his brother: two hundred new
letters.* Cobden-Sanderson, 1933
Bradford, Sarah, *George VI.* Weidenfeld & Nicolson, 1989
Bryant, Arthur, *English saga (1840–1940).* Collins, 1940
Buchanan, Meriel, *Queen Victoria's relations.* Collins, 1954
Carey, M.C., *Princess Mary.* Nisbet, 1922
Charlot, Monica, *Victoria, the young Queen.* Blackwell, 1991
Daiken, Leslie, *Children's toys throughout the ages.* Spring, 1963
Dalton, Hugh, *Call back yesterday: memoirs 1887–1931.* Frederick Muller,
1953

Donaldson, Frances, *Edward VIII*. Weidenfeld & Nicolson, 1974

Duff, David, *Albert and Victoria*. Frederick Muller, 1972

—— *Hessian tapestry*. Frederick Muller, 1967

—— *The shy Princess: the life of Her Royal Highness Princess Beatrice, the youngest daughter and constant companion of Queen Victoria*. Evans Bros, 1958

—— *Victoria travels: Journeys of Queen Victoria between 1830 and 1900, with extracts from her journal*. Frederick Muller, 1970

Epton, Nina, *Victoria and her daughters*. Weidenfeld & Nicolson, 1971

Esher, Reginald Baliol Brett, 2nd Viscount, *The influence of King Edward and essays on other subjects*. John Murray, 1915

Frankland, Noble, *Prince Henry, Duke of Gloucester*. Weidenfeld & Nicolson, 1980

Frith, William Powell, *My autobiography and reminiscences*, 2 vols. Bentley, 1887

Gore, John, *King George V: a personal memoir*. John Murray, 1941

Greville, Charles, *The Greville Memoirs, 1817–60*; (ed.) Lytton Strachey & Roger Fulford, 8 vols. Macmillan, 1938

Hannas, Linda, *The jigsaw book*. Hutchinson, 1981

Hibbert, Christopher, *The Illustrated London News social history of Victorian Britain*. Angus & Robertson, 1975

—— *Queen Victoria: A Personal History*. Harper Collins, 2000

Hough, Richard, *Louis and Victoria: the first Mountbattens*. Hutchinson, 1974

—— (ed.), *Advice to a grand-daughter: Letters from Queen Victoria to Princess Victoria of Hesse*. Heinemann, 1975

Hughes, M.V., *A London child of the 1870s*. Oxford University Press, 1934

Keppel, G.T., Earl of Albemarle, *Fifty years of my life*. Jarrold, 1877

Keppel, Sonia, *Edwardian daughter*. Hamish Hamilton, 1958

King, Stella, *Princess Marina: her life and times*. Cassell, 1969

Lee, Sir Sidney, *King Edward VII: a biography*, 2 vols. Macmillan, 1925–7

Leslie, Anita, *Edwardians in love*. Hutchinson, 1972

Longford, Elizabeth, *The royal house of Windsor*. Weidenfeld & Nicolson, 1974

—— *Victoria R.I.* Weidenfeld & Nicolson, 1964

—— (ed.), *Darling Loosy: letters to Princess Louise, 1856–1939*. Weidenfeld & Nicolson, 1991

Lyttelton, Lady, *Correspondence of Sarah Spencer, Lady Lyttelton, 1787–1870*; edited by her great-granddaughter The Hon. Mrs Hugh Wyndham. John Murray, 1912

McClintock, Mary Howard, *The Queen thanks Sir Howard: the life of Major-General Sir Howard Elphinstone, V.C., K.C.B., C.M.G.* John Murray, 1945

BIBLIOGRAPHY

Maas, Jeremy, *The Prince of Wales's wedding: the story of a picture*. Cameron & Tayleur/David & Charles, 1977

Magnus, Philip, *King Edward the Seventh*. John Murray, 1964

Mallet, Victor (ed.), *Life with Queen Victoria: Marie Mallet's letters from court 1887–1901*. John Murray, 1968

Marie, Queen of Roumania, *The story of my life*, 3 vols. Cassell, 1934–5

Marie Louise, Princess, *My memories of six reigns*. Evans Bros, 1956

Martin, Theodore, *The life of His Royal Highness the Prince Consort*, 5 vols. Smith, Elder, 1875–80

Matson, John, *Dear Osborne*. Hamish Hamilton, 1978

Millais, John Guille, *The life and letters of Sir John Everett Millais, President of the Royal Academy*. Methuen, 1905

Morgan, Kenneth O. (ed.), *Lloyd George family letters 1885–1936*. University of Wales Press/Oxford University Press, 1973

Mullen, Richard, & Munson, James, *Victoria: Portrait of a Queen*. BBC, 1987

Nicolson, Harold, *King George V: his life and reign*. Constable, 1952

—— *Diaries and Letters 1930–1939*, ed. Nigel Nicolson. Collins, 1966

Noel, Gerard, *Ena, Spain's English Queen*. Constable, 1984

—— *Princess Alice: Queen Victoria's forgotten daughter*. Constable, 1974

Ormond, Richard, & Blackett-Ord, Carol, *Franz Xavier Winterhalter and the courts of Europe 1830–70*. National Portrait Gallery, 1987

Pakula, Hannah, *An Uncommon Woman: The Empress Frederick*. Weidenfeld & Nicolson, 1996

Pimlott, Ben, *Hugh Dalton*. Jonathan Cape, 1985

Plumb, J.H., & Wheldon, Huw, *Royal heritage: the story of Britain's royal builders and collectors*. BBC, 1977

Pope-Hennessy, James, *Queen Mary, 1867–1953*. Allen & Unwin, 1959

Priestley, J.B., *The Edwardians*. Heinemann, 1970

Reid, Michaela, *Ask Sir James: Sir James Reid, personal physician to Queen Victoria and physician-in-ordinary to three monarchs*. Hodder & Stoughton, 1987

Roberts, Jane, *Royal artists: from Mary Queen of Scots to the present day*. Grafton, 1987

Rose, Clare, *Children's clothes*. Batsford, 1989

Rose, Kenneth, *King George V*. Weidenfeld & Nicolson, 1983

Rowell, George, *Queen Victoria goes to the theatre*. Elek, 1978

St Aubyn, Giles, *Edward VII, Prince and King*. Collins, 1979

—— *Queen Victoria: a portrait*. Sinclair-Stevenson, 1991

—— *The royal George: the life of Prince George, Duke of Cambridge*. Constable, 1963

Shattuck, Roger, *The banquet years: The arts in France 1885–1918*. Faber, 1959

Speaight, Richard N., *Memoirs of a Court Photographer*. Hurst & Blackett, 1926

Stanley, Lady Augusta, *Letters of Lady Augusta Stanley, a young lady at court 1849–1863*; (ed.) the Dean of Windsor & Hector Bolitho. Gerald Howe, 1927

'This brilliant year': Queen Victoria's Jubilee 1887. Royal Academy of Arts (exhibition catalogue), 1977

Turner, Michael, *Osborne House*. English Heritage, 1989

Van der Kiste, John, *Edward VII's children*. Alan Sutton, 1989

—— *George V's children*. Alan Sutton, 1991

—— *Princess Victoria Melita: Grand Duchess Cyril of Russia, 1876–1936*. Alan Sutton, 1991

—— *Queen Victoria's children*. Alan Sutton, 1986

Van der Kiste, John, and Jordaan, Bee, *Dearest Affie: Alfred, Duke of Edinburgh, Queen Victoria's second son*. Alan Sutton, 1984

Victoria, Queen, *The girlhood of Queen Victoria: a selection from Her Majesty's diaries between the years 1832 and 1840*; (ed.) Viscount Esher, 2 vols. John Murray, 1912

—— *Leaves from the journal of our life in the Highlands, from 1848 to 1861*. Smith & Elder, 1868

—— *Letters of Queen Victoria: a selection from Her Majesty's correspondence between the years 1837 and 1861*, (ed.) A.C. Benson & Viscount Esher, 3 vols. John Murray, 1907

—— *Letters of Queen Victoria, second series: a selection from Her Majesty's correspondence and journals between the years 1862 and 1885*; (ed.) G.E. Buckle, 3 vols. John Murray, 1926–8

—— *Letters of Queen Victoria, third series: a selection from Her Majesty's correspondence and journals between the years 1886 and 1901*; (ed.) G.E. Buckle, 3 vols. John Murray, 1930–2

—— *Further letters of Queen Victoria: from the archives of the house of Brandenburg-Prussia*; (ed.) Hector Bolitho. Thornton Butterworth, 1938

Victoria, Queen, & Victoria, Consort of Frederick III, *Dearest Child: letters between Queen Victoria and the Princess Royal, 1858–1861*; (ed.) Roger Fulford. Evans Bros, 1964

—— *Dearest Mama: private correspondence of Queen Victoria and the Crown Princess of Prussia, 1861–1864*; (ed.) Roger Fulford. Evans Bros, 1968

—— *Your dear letter: private correspondence of Queen Victoria and the Crown Princess of Prussia, 1865–1871*; (ed.) Roger Fulford. Evans Bros, 1971

—— *Darling child: private correspondence between Queen Victoria and the Crown Princess of Prussia, 1871–78*; (ed.) Roger Fulford. Evans Bros, 1976

—— *Beloved Mama: private correspondence of Queen Victoria and the German Crown Princess, 1878–1885*; (ed.) Roger Fulford. Evans Bros, 1981

—— *Beloved and darling child: last letters between Queen Victoria and her eldest daughter, 1886–1901*; (ed.) Agatha Ramm. Alan Sutton, 1990

BIBLIOGRAPHY

Victoria, Consort of Frederick III, *The Empress Frederick writes to Sophie, her daughter, Crown Princess and later Queen of the Hellenes: letters, 1889–1901*; (ed.) Arthur Gould Lee. Faber, 1955

—— *Letters of the Empress Frederick*, (ed.) Sir Frederick Ponsonby. Macmillan, 1928

Wake, Jehanne, *Princess Louise, Queen Victoria's unconventional daughter*. Collins, 1988

Warner, Marina, *Queen Victoria's sketchbook*. Macmillan, 1979

Warren, T. Herbert, *Christian Victor: the story of a young soldier*. John Murray, 1903

Weintraub, Stanley, *Victoria: biography of a Queen*. Unwin Hyman, 1987

—— *The importance of being Edward: King in Waiting 1841–1901*. John Murray, 2000

Wheeler-Bennett, John W., *King George VI: his life and reign*. Macmillan, 1958

Windsor, Duke of, *A family album*. Cassell, 1960

—— *A King's story: the memoirs of HRH the Duke of Windsor*. Cassell, 1951

Woodham-Smith, Mrs Cecil, *Queen Victoria, her life and times, Vol. 1, 1819–1861*. Hamish Hamilton, 1972

Ziegler, Philip, *King Edward VIII: the official biography*. Collins, 1990

—— *Mountbatten: the official biography*. Collins, 1985

III PERIODICALS

Daily Telegraph
Illustrated London News
Royalty Digest

Index

Note: major entries are in chronological order, where appropriate.

INDEX